U0114977

LISTENING

雅思听力突破

技巧与训练

陈佳琦　主编

基础版

上海财经大学出版社

图书在版编目 (CIP) 数据

雅思听力突破：技巧与训练：基础版 / 陈佳琦主
编． — 上海：上海财经大学出版社，2023.8
ISBN 978-7-5642-4236-7/F.4236

Ⅰ．①雅… Ⅱ．①陈… Ⅲ．① IELTS —听说教学—自
学参考资料 Ⅳ．① H319.9

中国国家版本馆 CIP 数据核字（2023）第 160421 号

□ 责任编辑 陈 佶
□ 封面设计 贺加贝

雅思听力突破——技巧与训练
（基础版）

陈佳琦 主 编

上海财经大学出版社出版发行
（上海市中山北一路 369 号 邮编 200083）
网 址：http://www.sufep.com
电子邮箱：webmaster @ sufep.com
全国新华书店经销
上海颛辉印刷厂有限公司印刷装订
2023 年 8 月第 1 版 2023 年 8 月第 1 次印刷

787mm×1092mm 1/16 12.25 印张 252 千字
定价：68.00 元

前　言

英语作为一种交际工具，在现代国际社会中起着举足轻重的作用。人们学习英语很重要的一个目的就是能够用英语自如地表达自己的思想，达到交际的目的。而交际是建立在听的基础上，因此，提高学生听的能力，是英语学习中必不可少的一个环节。它直接关系到说、读、写三种能力的提高，也是能否完成英语教学任务的关键。如何有效提高学生的英语听力，是一代代英语教学工作者不断探讨的难题。

《雅思听力突破——技巧与训练（基础版）》是为备战雅思考试的考生编写的一本听力基础教材。其目的在于循序渐进地训练和提高学生的英语听力技能。这本书是参照雅思听力为 3.5 ~ 4.5 分的学生的实际英语水平编写而成的。

雅思听力考试总时间为 40 分钟，共有 4 段语音。普通培训类和学术类听力题目完全一样，每段有 10 个问题，总共为 40 题左右，满分为 9 分。4 段听力内容的难度理论上逐步递增：

Section 1 是有关社会生活方面的话题。比如：咨询旅游方面的信息、参观一个新的城市、参加一个体育健身项目等。这段内容是由两个人对话构成的。

Section 2 仍然是有关社会生活方面的，但是却不是对话，而是一段独白。例如：一段新闻播报、公益活动的开场介绍等。

Section 3 是有关教育学术方面的话题。例如：几位学生在一起讨论某个课题、老师和学生一起的专题研讨等。这段内容一般是 2 ~ 4 人的谈话节目。

Section 4 话题同 Section 3，但和第二段听力内容相似，仍旧是一段独白。例如：一场大学讲座、公开演讲等。

题型多样化是雅思听力考试的一大特点，熟悉听力考试的题型是顺利通过考试的前提条件，很多水平很高的考生因为不适应多变的题型而无法取得理想的分数。在听力考试中，常见的题型主要有：

● 填表题（Forms / Notes / Table Completion）

● 单 / 多项选择题（Multiple Choice）

● 分类题（Classification）

● 连线题（Matching）

- 填空题（Gap-filling）

- 图表标注题（Labelling a Diagram / Plan / Map）

- 短问题回答（Short-answer Questions）

听力考试的每个 section 里都会出现 1—3 类不同的题型，用于考查考生获取细节的能力和对主要内容的理解能力。前者要求考生填写原文中出现的内容或者是相关的同义词，是考生比较容易得分的部分；后者对考生的实际水平有很高的要求，通常要求考生根据听到的大部分文章内容，自己总结出答案。

本教材内容新颖、题材广泛、题型多样，在练习方面，针对雅思考点做了精心设计：

1. 听懂并记住名字、地址、数字、时间等细节；

2. 理解专题词汇和习惯用语的意思；

3. 掌握事件的内在联系和因果关系等；

4. 理解文章的主旨大意；

5. 领会谈话者的观点、态度、感情和真实意图。

针对雅思的考试特点，本教材共编写了 10 个单元，依次为中低级、中级、中高级三个层次，分别供使用者在不同阶段使用。每个单元由 9 个部分组成，包括专题词汇听写热身、专题知识介绍、常见雅思考点、词汇积累、基础练习、听力技巧讲解、速记练习、专题练习和文化介绍。本教材录音以标准的美国音或英国音为主，声音清晰；练习形式活泼，其设计参考了雅思考试的形式，并增加了是非题、填充题、听写、讲座摘记和根据笔记回答问题等多种形式。最后的文化介绍不仅能够为教师备课提供必要的历史文化背景，也可以作为学生的课外阅读材料，以扩大学生的知识面。本教材适合课堂教学，也便于雅思考生自学，同样适用于具有相当听力水平的英语专业和非英语专业的学生及广大的英语爱好者。

需要特别说明的是，依据国家教材委员会办公室《关于做好党的二十大精神进教材工作的通知》（国教材办〔2022〕3 号）的要求，推动党的二十大精神进教材、进课堂、进头脑，除了本教材中已经体现的相关内容外，为了与时俱进地增补与本教材相关的思政案例与二十大精神内容，及时修改在教学过程中发现的本书错误之处，我们与出版社共同建设新媒体动态服务窗口，使用本教材的教师可以通过手机 QQ 扫封底二维码，获取练习答案、录音音频、录音稿及其他相关最新内容。由于作者水平有限，书中必有纰漏和错误之处，敬请使用者指教，以便修正。

陈佳琦

2023.7

Contents

Objectives:

● to know the origin of English names

● to know the spelling of common names

● to know the special meaning of some English names

● to practice the pronunciation of vowels

● to know the English characters

I. Warm up

Exercise 1: Dictation of Words

1. _____	6. _____	11. _____	16. _____
2. _____	7. _____	12. _____	17. _____
3. _____	8. _____	13. _____	18. _____
4. _____	9. _____	14. _____	19. _____
5. _____	10. _____	15. _____	20. _____

✿ II. Background Information—Names [1]

When we learn a foreign language and try to make effective communication, we need to know about names and naming, just as when we study a language we need to know its vocabulary and its grammar. Personal names are not only linguistic symbols that distinguish one person from others, but also social symbols, representing relationships in societies and cultures. Though studying the characteristics and origins of English names and cultural influence on English names, we can know more about English names and thus remember an English name more easily and learn some English culture at the same time.

● The components of English names

What is a name? The *Longman Dictionary of Contemporary English* defines the word name as "the word that someone or something is known by", "but a name goes deeper than that". A person's name serves as their identity for the rest of the life.

An English name mostly have three parts including first name (Christian name, given name, baptismal name), middle name (second name) and last name (family name, surname).

● Titles

Miss/Mrs./Ms.	chief engineer 总工程师	vice president 副总统
Mr.	head coach 主教练	vice governor 副州长
Dr.	secretary-general 秘书长	vice mayor 副市长
Prof.	honorary president 荣誉校长	associate professor 副教授
Sir	deputy dean 副院长	senior engineer 高级工程师

● Origins of last names

Generally speaking, family names have six origins. They may develop from surroundings, occupations, statues or titles, personal characteristics or human bodies. Last but not least, a lot of last names comes from fathers.

➢ **Surroundings**

Many English-speaking nations use the names of their birth places or living places as their surnames, such as Ellington, Ford, London, Scott, etc. Also, there are some surnames originating

---

1 https://wenku.baidu.com/view/ae37419d3186bceb18e8bb3b.html?_wkts_=1668650335969

from topography and scenery, such as Lake, Lock, Brook, River, Cape, Hall, Hill, Pond, etc.

➤ Occupations

In the late middle ages, the social economy in England gradually developed, many English people use their occupation as their surnames, many of which were passed down, such as Archer, Carter, and Potter.

➤ Statues or titles

Some noble families use their title as their surnames to show off, such as Constable, Judge, King, Marshall, etc.

➤ Personal characteristics or human bodies

There are some surnames originating from the words used to describe people's appearance, physiological trait, temperament, and human body, such as Armstrong, Boon, Black, Longfellow, Short, Young, Wise, Arms, Cheek, Back, Temple, etc.

➤ Fathers' names

Most of these names end with "son". The structure is "father's name or its variant +son", such as Addison (son of Adam), Anderson (son of Andrew), Thomason (son of Thomas), Williamson (son of William), and Wilson (son of Will). What worth mentioning is that such patronymic surnames as Richardson, Robinson, and Williamson were gradually shortened into Richards, Robins and Williams. So we know Richard, Robin, and William are all first name, while Richards, Robins, and Williams are all family names.

➤ Patronymic names

Patronymic names means names derived from parent or ancestor. The patronymic last names are common in most languages. French word Fitz serves the same purpose as son and appears in some modern English names, such as Fitzgerald, Fitzsimmons. Among Scotch and Irish the word with the same function is Mac. It means relatives. The Irish letter O acts as the same function as Mac/Mc. For example, O'Neil means son of Neil.

➤ Culture influence on names

The development of English names is a component part of English culture, which catches the same step with human civilization. English names help the development of culture and at the same time culture promote the names to move forward. Culture including Christianity, history and literature influence English names deeply.

➤ **Christianity influence on names**

Jesus Christ has 12 disciples such as Mathew, Peter, James, etc., all of their names are common except the rebel Juda. According to the statistics of personal names in the 12th century, there were 1% of people named John. And according to the statistics of personal names in 13th century, there were 25% of people named John.

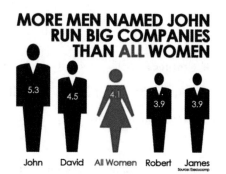

The feminine sages' names also are popular first names such as, Mary (Jesus Christ's mother), Ann (Mary's mother), and Catherine (Peter's wife). People also often like to select the sages' names in the Old Testament such as Noah (the man who made the Noah and took each kind of animal into it), Abraham (the founder of Judaism), Sarah (Abraham's wife), etc. By the 17th century, all names appear in Holy Bible were used, and now, they are still very common.

➤ **History influence on names**

Surnames with the prefix "o" have the Irish characteristic. There are also many Irish surnames beginning with Mul, for example, Mulcahy and Mulligan. Those names beginning with Mac or Mc are usually Scottish surnames. For instance, McArthur, MacDonald, McMichael, or McMillan may well be the surname of a Scot or of a person whose ancestor was from Scotland. Surnames of Welsh developed after the English king Henry 8th, and most of them originated from French, Old English and Hebrew. Such as Hugo, Hughs, etc. are all common surnames. Some familiar English and Welsh surnames like Edwards, Jones, Owen, Thomas and Williams, are of Welsh origin.

➤ **Literature influence on names**

Many people in English-speaking countries have been influenced by literature when they choose names for themselves or their children.

Many names from literature have specific meanings, and they are called "meaningful name". One example is Robinson which is the hero of Robinson Crusoe by Daniel Defoe who fight against with nature to survive. This name gradually become a symbol of brave, strength and power, which is loved by parents to name their boys.

Speaking Practice: Read the Following Names [1]

Proper Names for Different People

Constellations	For Males	For Females
1. 白羊座（Aries）	Charles, Mark, Bill, Vincent, William, Joseph, James	Malcolm, Joan, Niki, Betty, Linda, Whitney, Lily
2. 双鱼座（Pisces）	Albert, Kevin, Michael, Taylor, Jackson, Jack, Jimmy	Elizabeth, Kelly, May, Julie, Amanda, Fiona
3. 金牛座（Taurus）	Fred, Gary, William, Charles, Michael, Karl	Barbara, Elizabeth, Helen, Katharine, Lee, Ann, Diana
4. 双子座（Gemini）	Bob, John, Thomas, Dean, Paul, Jack, Brooke	Judy, Doris, Rudy, Amanda, Shirley, Joan, Tracy
5. 巨蟹座（Cancer）	Kevin, Louis, John, George, Henry, Benjamin	Melody, Helen, Debbie, Lisa, Yvonne
6. 狮子座（Leo）	Robert, Carl, Scott, Tom, Eddy, Kris, Peter	Shelly, Mary, Dolly, Nancy, Jane, Barbara
7. 处女座（Virgo）	Johnson, Bruce, Robert, Peter, Bill, Joseph, John	Shirley, Emily, Sophia, Vivian, Lillian, Joy
8. 天秤座（Libra）	Burt, Charlie, Elliot, George, Johnson	Ross, Julie, Gloria, Carol
9. 天蝎座（Scorpio）	Richard, James, Charles, Bruce, David	Taylor, Wendy, Grace, Vivian, Caroline, Samantha
10. 射手座（Sagittarius）	Nick, Walt, John, Mark, Sam, Davis, Neil, Carl	Maria, Kate, Demi, Sunny, Wendy
11. 摩羯座（Capricorn）	Richard, Howard Allen, Johnny, Robert, Martin, Jeff	Ava, Christina, Judy, Susan, Grace, Alice
12. 水瓶座（Aquarius）	Paul, Sam, Francis, Lewis, Stephen, Andy, Scott	Joyce, Sally, Margaret, Rebecca, Teresa, Rita, Jessica

How to read these names [2]:

Ann—Anne—Annie	Thomas	Jose [hoʊˈzeɪ]
David	Sophia	Stephen=Steven
Tony	Taylor—Tyler	Keith [iː]
Richard	Sean=Shawn	Ivan
Zoe	Leonard [lenəd]	Ethan

1　https://wenku.baidu.com/view/90039843aa8271fe910ef12d2af90242a895ab64.html?wkts=1668650828414

2　https://mp.weixin.qq.com/s?_biz=MjM5MTAwMzY0Ng==&mid=2657548894&idx=3&sn=5e258e45 f69487275ac2a2f7f5f5b669&chksm=bd2e7ccf8a59f5d98ec7cf8398f9fa0bd8b93641adda523b3f4cc2c cb0422b98ba23408609a3&scene=27

❧ III. Testing Key Points

雅思听力考试中，尤其是 Part 1，经常考到人名的拼写，除此以外，还有各种演出的名字、公司机构的名字、景点的名称等，有些在录音里会有拼读，有些则没有；有些拼写和读音比较规律，有些则不然（主要是因为外来词、非英语单词）。这要求考生注意听音和拼写，同时还要注意大写等事项。常考的名字类具体表现为：

1. 人名——申请人、被访者、联系人、客户、求职者等

2. 机构名称——公司、俱乐部等

3. 节目名称——话剧、音乐、木偶剧等

4. 站点名称——火车站、地铁站等

5. 地点名称——景点、公园、剧场、博物馆等

6. 建筑名称——公寓、图书馆等

注意：

➢ 每个单词首字母都要大写

➢ 字母拼读要听清楚，分清 b, d, p, t, j, g 等

➢ 可能有 double l 或 double u，不要听成 w

➢ 'a' for apple 这样的表达是为了明确哪个字母

❧ IV. Word Bank

Names in IELTS [1]:

1. Males

Andrew 安德鲁	Dennis 丹尼斯	Jason 杰森	Robert 罗伯特
Bill 比尔	Frank 富兰克	Kevin 凯文	Thomas 托马斯
Bob 鲍勃	Henry 亨利	Mark 马克	William 威廉
David 大卫	James 詹姆斯	Mike 麦克	

2. Females

Barbara 芭芭拉	Jane 珍	Lisa 丽莎	Sarah 莎拉
Ellen 艾伦	Joan 琼	Susan 苏珊	Helen 海伦
Mary 玛丽	Wendy 温蒂		

1　http://www.xz-edu.com/lang/content-0-39886.html

✦ V. Basic Training

Exercise 2: Abbreviations and Spelling [1]

Listen to the recordings and write down the words you hear.

Abbreviations:

1.　　　　　2.　　　　　3.　　　　　4.　　　　　5.　　　　　6.

Spelling:

1.　　　　　2.　　　　　3.　　　　　4.

5.　　　　　6.　　　　　7.　　　　　8.

Exercise 3: Listening Activity [2]

Listen to some dialogues between a caller on the phone and a secretary. As you listen write the names in the spaces below.

1. Is that 4013745?

   Yes. Can I help you?

   I'd like to speak to _____, please.

2. Hi. Is that 2016453?

   Yes. Who do you want to speak to?

   _____, please.

3. Hello. Is that 7849253?

   Who do you wish to speak to?

   _____, please.

4. Good morning. Is that 5066423?

   Yes. Can I help you?

   I'd like to speak to _____, please.

5. I'm sorry to disturb you, but is that 5094287?

   Who do you wish to speak to?

   _____, please.

1　何其莘 编：《Listen to this 1》，外语教学与研究出版社，2002 年：第 1 页

2　李亚宾 编著：《IELTS 考试技能训练教程：听力》，北京语言大学出版社，2007 年：第 4 页

Exercise 4: Write down the Names and Places You Hear

1.   2.   3.   4.

5.   6.   7.   8.

Exercise 5 [1]

A. Write down T if the statement is true and write down F if the statement is false after you hear the conversation.

1. It is the first time Mr. Thomas and Mr. Simmons have met.

2. Mr. Simmons lives in Singapore.

3. Ms. Goodhall is a sales director.

4. Mr. Thomas has been to London before.

5. They will all meet again in Singapore next year.

B. Answer the questions according to the conversation you hear.

6. When did Mr. Thomas arrive?

_____

7. Which section does Mr. Thomas work for?

_____

8. Who showed Mr. Thomas around London last year?

_____

9. Where is the next trade show?

_____

10. When is the next trade show?

_____

VI. Listening Skill 1—Phonetics (Vowels)

英语音标表（英语国际音标表，dj 音标）		
单元音	短元音	[i] [ə] [ɔ] [u] [ʌ] [e] [æ]
	长元音	[i:] [ə:] [ɔ:] [u:] [ɑ:]

---

1 上田真理砂 & Iain Davey 著，葛窈君 译：《听见英国——英式英语实境听力练习》，众文图书公司，2021 年：第 113 页

Continued

双元音		[ei] [ai] [ɔi] [au] [əu] [iə] [ɛə] [uə]
清浊成对的辅音	清辅音	[p] [t] [k] [f] [θ] [s] [ts] [tr] [ʃ] [tʃ]
	浊辅音	[b] [d] [g] [v] [ð] [z] [dz] [dr] [ʒ] [dʒ]
其他辅音		[h] [m] [n] [ŋ] [l] [r] [j] [w]

Pronunciations [1]

➢ 注意发音的要点，舌位和口型

➢ 注意字母以及字母组合一般发音规律

➢ 注意区分元音的发音

➢ 注意重读的位置

➢ 注意弱读、连读、失爆、连辅等发音特点

➢ 注意发音和拼写规律

➢ 注意英音、美音、澳音、法音、印度音、日本音、泰国音等区别

1. 元音 e 的特殊发音单词

（1）元音 e 发 a

genre 英 ['ʒɒ̃rə] n. 类型，种类；体裁，样式；风俗画

（2）发音 ei

cafe ['kæfeɪ]

（3）e 也可以发音为 i:（并不一定与 ee、ea 组合一起才发音 i:）

athlete ['æθliːt] n. 运动员，体育家；身强力壮的人。元音 e 发 [iː]

sequel ['siːkwəl] n.（书、电影、戏剧等的）续篇，续集；后续的事；结果

prequel ['priːkwəl] n. 先篇，前篇，前传（叙述某流行图书或电影中的故事之前的事情）

（4）不发音（不在结尾）

clothes [kləʊðz] 很多人发成 [kləʊðiz]，这里的 e 是不发音的

vegetable ['vedʒtəbl] 第二个 e 是不发音的，很多人说成了 [vedʒitəbl]

（5）在结尾发音

Nike ['naɪki]

finale 英 [fɪ'nɑːli] n. 终曲；结局，大团圆；最后一场

---

1 http://www.okeyen.com/a/listensay/13.html

2. 元音 a 的特殊发音单词

cater ['keɪtə(r)] 很多人 a 发成了 æ，估计是受单词 caterpillar 的影响，a 在开音节中发 [eɪ]

bathing ['beɪðɪŋ] bath [bɑːθ]

3. 元音 i 的特殊发音单词

元音 i 在以 e 结尾的单词中重读一般都是发 ai 的音，但也有例外：expertise [ˌekspər'tiz]

Pronunciation Practice [1]

1. Read the phonetics

(1) phenomenon [fɪ'nɒmɪnən] n. 现象

(2) anaesthetist [ə'nisθətɪst] n. 麻醉师

(3) remuneration [rɪˌmjuːnə'reɪʃ(ə)n] n. 报酬

(4) statistics [stə'tɪstɪks] n. 统计

(5) ethnicity [eθ'nɪsɪtɪ] n. 种族划分

(6) philosophical [fɪlə'sɒfɪk(ə)l] adj. 哲学的

(7) provocatively [prəu'vɒkətɪvlɪ] adv. 煽动地

(8) anonymous [ə'nɒnɪməs] adj. 匿名的

(9) thesaurus [θɪ'sɔːrəs] n. 宝库；辞典

(10) aluminium [æl(j)ʊ'mɪnɪəm] adj. 铝的

2. Read the words

(1) seat—sit	(6) book—boot	(11) crush—crash
(2) neat—knit	(7) should—shoe	(12) cat—cart
(3) said—sad	(8) foot—food	(13) dull—doll
(4) spot—sport	(9) mud—mad	(14) wonder—wander
(5) pot—port	(10) fun—fan	(15) duck—dock

3. Read the phrases

(1) sit in this seat	(5) cool the soup	(8) the railway station
(2) a bit of peas	(6) full of good rules	(9) the train in waiting
(3) run back to get the cat	(7) the rain in Spain	(10) try nine times
(4) had a fan in her left hand		

1　https://m.hujiang.com/en_fanyi/p565526/

4. Tongue twist

(1) A good beginning makes a good ending.

(2) The leaf of this vine is very fine.

(3) There are other things worth thinking about.

(4) A penny saved is a penny earned.

(5) Now things are beginning to swing.

✍ VII. Note-taking Practice

Exercise 6: Listen and copy [1]

1. This weekend is certain to be enjoyable.

_____

2. Things will work out fine.

_____

3. She'll be great, I'm sure.

_____

4. Tom is bound to win it.

_____

5. I have no doubt of his success.

_____

6. You're bound to enjoy.

_____

7. The party is bound to be successful.

_____

8. Everything will be good, I'm sure.

_____

1　闫先凤 编：《听力密码：听见英国》，中国水利水电出版社，2019 年：第 45 页

Exercise 7: Listen and write [1]

1. _____

2. _____

3. _____

4. _____

5. _____

6. _____

7. _____

8. _____

VIII. Target Training

Exercise 8: VOA special—All about the names [2]

Listen to the recording and fill in the blanks below.

A person's name is very important. Some names also have special meanings in popular American expressions. To better understand what I mean, sit back and listen. You might even want to get a cup of 1. _____, I mean, a cup of coffee.

One day, an average 2. _____ was walking down the street. An average 3. _____ is a common person—either male or female. This average 4. _____ was lost. He did not know 5. _____ about where he was going. By this, I mean he did not know anything about where to find things in the city.

So average 6. _____ asked 7. _____ for directions to the nearest bank. 8. _____ is also a common person—male or female.

"9. _____," said 10. _____. This is an expression of surprise. "11. _____, don't you know that all banks are closed today? It is Saturday."

1 闫先凤 编：《听力密码：听见英国》，中国水利水电出版社，2019 年：第 50 页
2 https://www.tingclass.net/show-8394-252719-1.html?gfh

"For 12. _____ sake," said average 13. _____. This is also an expression used to show a feeling like surprise or disappointment.

"For 14. _____ sake. I do not believe you," said average 15. _____. He was being a doubting 16. _____, someone who does not believe anything he is told.

At that moment, 17. _____ was walking down the street with a woman. 18. _____ is also an expression for a common man. Now this 19. _____ was NOT walking next to a plain 20. _____. A plain 21. _____ is a woman who is neither ugly nor pretty. She is simply plain. No, the woman with 22. _____ was a real 23. _____ — a beautiful woman.

Average 24. _____ asked the woman if all banks were closed on Saturday. "No way, 25. _____," she answered. This is a way of saying "no." "No way, 26. _____. Many banks are open on Saturdays."

Average 27. _____ did not know either of these two people from 28. _____. That is, he did not know them at all. But he followed their directions to the nearest bank.

When he arrived, he walked to the desk of the chief bank employee. Now this man was a true 29. _____ of all trades. He knew how to do everything.

"I am here to withdraw some money so I can pay my taxes to Uncle 30. _____," said average 31. _____. Uncle 32. _____ represents the United States government. The banker produced some papers and told average 33. _____ to sign his 34. _____ at the bottom. A 35. _____ is a person's signed name—a signature. Historically, 36. _____ was one of the signers of the United States *Declaration of Independence*. 37. _____ had a beautiful signature and signed his name larger than all the others.

As average 38. _____ left the bank he began to sing. But sadly, average 39. _____ was not a good singer. He was a 40. _____ One Note. He could only sing one note.

Exercise 9: Choosing A Name [1]

Listen to the recording and complete the summary and the table below with ONLY ONE WORD AND/OR A NUMBER.

Children seem to identify especially strongly with their names. A quarter young children feel they would not exist anymore without their name. About 1. _____ of all young people wish they could be given a different name.

Some people choose to change their names when they grow up, for example, people in

2. _____ business because they wanted their names to sound 3. _____ for the work.

Cultures will influence people to choose a name. For example, a name that has been in their family for many years gives the child a sense of 4. _____. But other parents create a completely new word to name their new baby.

Name	Meaning	Name	Meaning	Name	Meaning
Nathaniel	given by God	Mosi in Africa	a first born 9. _____	Malak	angel
Wunand	God is 5. _____	Kazuo in 10. _____	first born	Mahira	quick and full of 13. _____
Edith	valuable 6. _____	Ama in Africa	born on 11. _____	Cahil	lack 14. _____
Amanda	worthy of 7. _____	Huyu in China	born in 12. _____	Huang	15. _____
Fara	cause for 8. _____			Fahim	intelligent

---

1   https://www.tingclass.net/show-8483-255786-1.html

IX. Listen and Understand the Culture

Exercise 10: Listen, Read and Speak

The English Character[1]
英国人的性格

To other Europeans, the best known quality of the British, and in particular of the English, is "reserved". A reserved person is one who does not talk very much to strangers, does not show much emotion，and seldom gets excited. It is difficult to get to know a reserved person: he never tells you anything about himself, and you may work with him for years without ever knowing where he lives, how many children he has, and what his interests are. English people tend to be like that.

在其他欧洲人看来，英国人，尤其是英格兰人最明显的特点是"沉默寡言"。一个沉默寡言的人不太同陌生人说话，情感不太外露，也很少激动。要想了解一个沉默寡言的人很困难：他从不谈及他的身世，即使你与他工作数年，也许你不知道他家住在哪里、有几个子女、有些什么兴趣爱好。英国人往往就是这样。

If they are making a journey by bus they will do their best to find an empty seat; if by train, an empty compartment. If they have to share the compartment with a stranger, they may travel many miles without starting a conversation. If a conversation does start, personal questions like "How old are you?" or even "What is your name?" are not easily asked.

乘公共汽车旅行时，他们会尽量找到一个空座位；乘火车旅行时，他们会尽量找到一个空隔间。如果他们不得不与他人共坐一个隔间，火车开了数英里也许还不见他们开口说话。即使打开了话匣子，他们也不轻易问起"你多大了？"或者"你贵姓？"之类的个人问题。

This reluctance to communicate with others is an unfortunate quality in some ways since it tends to give the impression of coldness, and it is true that the English (except perhaps in the North) are not noted for their generosity and hospitality.

从某些方面来说，这种不愿与人交往的特点是件令人遗憾的事情，因为这往往给人以冷漠的印象。（除了北方人以外）英国人从不以他们的慷慨大方和热情好客而著称。

1　闫先凤 编：《听力密码：听见英国》，中国水利水电出版社，2019 年：第 161 页

On the other hand, they are perfectly human behind their barrier of reserve and may be quite pleased when a friendly stranger or foreigner succeeds for a time in breaking the barrier down. We may also mention at this point that the people the North and West, especially the Welsh, are much less reserved than those of the South and East.

另一方面，虽然他们表面上沉默寡言，但内心还是很有人情味的。当友善的陌生人或外国人打破沉默时，他们也许会感到很高兴。说到这里，也许我们应该提一句，英国的北部和西部的人，特别是威尔士人，远不像南部和东部的人那样缄默。

Closely related to English reserve is English modesty. Within their hearts, the English are perhaps no less conceited than anybody else, but in their relations with others they value at least a show of modesty. Self-praise is felt to be impolite.

与英国人的缄默密切相关的是英国人的谦虚。在英国人的内心，他们的自负不亚于任何其他的民族。但在与别人交往时，他们注重谦虚，起码要表现出一种谦虚的姿态。自夸被认为是不礼貌的。

If a person is, let us say, very good at tennis and someone asks him if he is a good player, he will seldom reply "Yes," because people will think him conceited. He will probably give an answer like, "I'm not bad," or "I think I'm very good," or "Well, I'm very keen on tennis." (i.e. I'm very fond of it.) Even if he had managed to reach the finals in last year's local championships, he would say it in such a way as to suggest that it was only due to a piece of good luck.

比如说，一个人网球打得很好，当有人问他是不是一个网球高手时，他很少会回答说"是"，因为如果他回答"是"，人们会认为他很自负。他很可能会这样回答"还不错"或者"我觉得我还行"或者"嗯，我挺喜欢打网球"。即使他在去年当地的网球锦标赛上打入了决赛，他也许会说只是碰上了好运气。

The famous English sense of humor is similar. Its starting-point is self-dispraise, and its great enemy is conceit. Its object is the ability to laugh at oneself—at one's own faults, one's own failure, even at one's own ideals. The criticism, "He has sense of humor" is very commonly heard in Britain, where humor is highly prized.

　　著名的英国式幽默也与此相似。其出发点是自贬，其大敌是自负。其目的是能够自嘲——嘲笑自己的错误、自己的失败，甚至是自己的理想。在英国，幽默感受到高度重视，经常听到"他没有幽默感"这样的评论。

What have you learnt from this passage?

1. New words

_____

_____

_____

2. Summary

_____

_____

_____

3. Your opinion

_____

_____

_____

Numbers and Measurements

Objectives:

● to know the numbers, including cardinal number, ordinal number decimal, fraction and percentage, and measures

● to know the spelling of units of measurements

● to learn about some news with numbers

● to practice the pronunciation of consonants

● to know the British Etiquette

5		7	2				3	6
6					8			7
1	3					2		
							9	
	7	3	9			4	6	8
9		1			2		7	5
	9			6			8	
	1						4	3
			4	5	8		6	

✤ I. Warm up

Exercise 1: Dictation of Words

1. _____   6. _____   11. _____   16. _____

2. _____   7. _____   12. _____   17. _____

3. _____   8. _____   13. _____   18. _____

4. _____   9. _____   14. _____   19. _____

5. _____   10. _____   15. _____   20. _____

❧ II. Background Information

Part I　Numbers

1. cardinal number

Number 1 to 100 are the very basic elements for all the number combinations. The more you get familiar with, the better you understand. And you also need to know hundred, thousand, million, and billion.

Speaking Practice: Please read the numbers below.

A. 917	B. 6,067	C. 816	D. 3,100	E. 424
F. 5,706	G. 381	H. 3,308	I. 6,936	J. 886
K. 7,323	L. 299	M.578	N. 7,822	O. 245

Special "0" —zero, oh, nought [nɔt], null

2. ordinal number

To spell ordinal numbers, just add -th to cardinal numbers, such as fourth and sixteenth. There are exceptions: **first, second, third, fifth, eighth, ninth, and twelfth**. When expressed as figures, the last two letters of the written word are added to the ordinal number.

3. decimal, fraction and percentage

● How to pronounce decimals

We list some sentences containing decimals and percentage. The number zero ("0") in decimals is usually pronounced as "zero." We pronounce 0.1 as zero-point-one, or point-one without zero in a casual or informal manner.

an example of decimals

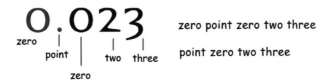

zero point zero two three

point zero two three

- How to pronounce fractions

Here is an example of mixed fractions. If the numerator is more than one, the denominator is plural, adding s as a suffix.

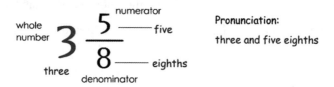

an example of mixed fractions

whole number — three
numerator — five
denominator — eighths

Pronunciation:
three and five eighths

an example of large fractions

$\dfrac{15}{20}$ — fifteen — twentieths

Three ways to pronounce a large fraction:
fifteen twentieths
fifteen over twenty
fifteen divided by twenty

➢ **Special ways to pronounce a fraction:**
   √ Nine in ten people
   √ Nine out of ten people
   √ Nine every ten people

- How to pronounce percentages

25 % (twenty-five percent)   99% (ninety-nine percent)

➢ **Special ways to pronounce a percentage:**
   a quarter, a half, three quarters, two and a half percent

- How to pronounce telephone numbers

(818) 252-7700 (seven-seven-oh-oh; double seven double oh)

Exercise 2: Please Read the Following Telephone Numbers

853-4967   (520) 864-6599   (646) 938-2165

(917) 642-8073   (212) 296-4801   1-800-555-1616

NB: double, triple, three 8s, four 3s

Part II Measurements

- **Linear Measure**

inch（英寸）   1 mile（英里）=1,760 yards   decimeter

1 foot（英尺）=12 inches   millimeter   meter

1 yard（码）=3 feet   centimeter   kilometer

- **Square/Cubic Measure**

square/cubic inch（平方 / 立方英寸）   acre（英亩）

square/cubic foot（平方 / 立方英尺）   hectare（公顷）

square/cubic yard（平方 / 立方码）   square mile（平方英里）

- **Capacity Measure**

1 pint（品脱）= 0.568 litre（升）   1 quart（夸脱）= 2 pints

1 gallon（加仑）= 4 quarts   1 bushel（蒲式耳）= 4 pecks（配克）

1 peck = 2 gallons   1 quarter（夸特）= 8 bushels

- **Weight Measure**

milligram（毫克）   gram（克）   kilogram（千克）   pound（磅）   ton(nes)（公吨）

- **Money Measure**

$ dollar, cent   £ pound, penny/pence   € euro, euro cent

- **Speed Measure**

mph= mile(s) per hour   m/s

- **Temperature Measure**

Celsius degree（℃）   Fahrenheit degree（℉）   Kelvin

III. Testing Key Points

1. 电话号码，门牌号码，房间号码，邮编、银行卡号，课程代码，航班号，车次，座位号

2. 金额：餐费，住宿费，房租，押金，票价，折扣，工资，课程费用，保险费，物品价格

3. 时间：见下一单元

4. 长度、距离、速度、重量、面积、温度

5. 人数、年龄、门票张数

6. 字数

IV. Word Bank

1. telephone	8. fee/cost/expenditure	15. square
2. room number	9. rent	16. hectare
3. post code	10. deposit	17. temperature
4. bank account	11. fare	18. age
5. course code	12. distance	19. maximum/up to
6. flight number	13. kilometer	20. minimum/at least
7. bus/train/seat	14. area	21. word limit

V. Basic Training[1]

Exercise 3: Practice with Numbers 1

Listen to the recording and write down what you have heard on the tape.

A. Numbers:

1.   2.   3.   4.

5.   6.   7.   8.

B. Telephone numbers:

1.   2.   3.   4.

1　https://www.tingclass.net/show-6697-114772-1.html

Exercise 4: Practice with Numbers 2

Listen to the tape and write down the numbers. Please use "," to divide the long numbers. (eg. 158,020)

1. _____	6. _____	11. _____	16. _____
2. _____	7. _____	12. _____	17. _____
3. _____	8. _____	13. _____	18. _____
4. _____	9. _____	14. _____	
5. _____	10. _____	15. _____	

Exercise 5: Practice with Numbers 3

**A. Numbers. Look at the questions listed below and fill in the correct mileage. Please use ","
to divide the long numbers. The first one has been done for you.**

1. How far is it from Los Angeles to Chicago?   Answer: ___2,054___ miles.

2. How far is it from Houston to Miami?   Answer: _____ miles.

3. How far is it from Detroit to New York?   Answer: _____ miles.

4. How far is it from Miami to Los Angeles?   Answer: _____ miles.

5. How far is it from Detroit to Houston?   Answer: _____ miles.

**B. Numbers. Answer the following questions according to what you hear on the tape. Please
use "," to divide the long numbers. The first one has been done for you.**

1. What's the population of Cairo?   Answer: 5,400,000

2. What's the population of London?   Answer: _____

3. What's the population of New York?   Answer: _____

4. What's the population of Tokyo?   Answer: _____

5. What's the population of Sao Paulo?   Answer: _____

C. Numbers. Dictate the names of coins to get yourself familiarized with these terms.

Coins. How much do you know about the following? In American currency:

(a) a penny = 1 cent   (b) a nickel = 5 cents   (c) a dime = 10 cents   (d) a quarter = 25 cents

1. 1 dime   2.   3.   4.   5.

Exercise 6: Listening Activity [1]

Listen to some dialogues between a caller on the phone and a secretary. As you listen write the telephone numbers in the spaces below.

1. Is that _____?

   Yes. Can I help you?

   I'd like to speak to Miss Johns, please.

2. Hi. Is that _____?

   Yes. Who do you want to speak to?

   Helen Parker, please.

3. I'm sorry to disturb you, but is that _____?

   Who do you wish to speak to?

   Jane Casting, please.

4. Hello. Is that _____?

   Who do you wish to speak to?

   Dr. Robinson, please.

5. Good morning. Is that _____?

   Yes. Can I help you?

   I'd like to speak to Mr. Egge, please.

1 李亚宾 编著：《IELTS 考试技能训练教程——听力》，北京语言大学出版社，2007 年：第 4 页

❧ VI. Listening Skill 2—Phonetics (Consonants)[1]

● Phonetic symbol—Consonants

英语音标表（英语国际音标表，dj 音标）		
单元音	短元音	[i] [ə] [ɔ] [u] [ʌ] [e] [æ]
	长元音	[iː] [əː] [ɔː] [uː] [ɑː]
双元音		[ei] [ai] [ɔi] [au] [əu] [iə] [ɛə] [uə]
清浊成对的辅音	清辅音	[p] [t] [k] [f] [θ] [s] [ts] [tr] [ʃ] [tʃ]
	浊辅音	[b] [d] [g] [v] [ð] [z] [dz] [dr] [ʒ] [dʒ]
其他辅音		[h] [m] [n] [ŋ] [l] [r] [j] [w]

● Pronunciations

1. 错误发音

● Receipt 发票　×Ree-sipt [rɪ'sept]　　√Ree-seet [rɪ'sit]

　p 是不发音的

● Debt 债务　×[debt] 单词中的字母 b 是不发音的　　√[det]

● Suite 套房　×[sut] 和 "suit" 不一样　　√[swit] 发音居然与 "sweet" 类似！

● App 应用　不要单个字母读成 "A-P-P"，√读作 [æp]，"App" 是 "application" 的缩写，同样的还有 PPT

● sergeant 英 ['sɑːdʒənt] n. [军] 军士，中士；警官，巡官；高级律师；注意 er 发 [ɑː]。再比如：clerk

● unwind 英 [ʌn'waɪnd] vt. 展开，从缠绕中解开；（使）心情轻松；vi. 放松，解开，松开；这里 i 发 [aɪ] 的音，所以不要把 wind (v.) 读成了 [wind] (n.)

● nature & natural　注意 a 的发音，nature 发 [ei]，natural 发 [æ]

● chef　英 [ʃef]，注意区分 chef 和 chief

2. 重音位置

（1）同源词——不同词性，不同词意——注意重音后移

　　Photography, photographer, photographs 这几个单词的重音位置，两个 o 的发音可要注意了，前两个类似，后一个差别大。再比如，humiliate, humiliation；necessary, necessity [nə'ses.ə.ti] 必需品；technique [tek'niːk], technical

---

1　http://www.okeyen.com/a/listensay/13.html

（2）同形不同音——动词名词重音位置

　　有的两个音节的词可以是动词又是名词，一般来说动词重音在第二个音节，名词在第一个音节，如：address, record, permit, survey, suspect, present, content, compact, insert。但是也有例外：respect 重音都在第二个音节，access 重音都在第一个音节，register 重音都在第一个音节。

（3）其他：breath & breathe　　cartoon & canteen　　Seoul & soul　　expert, expect, except

● Pronunciation practice

1. Read the phonetics

(1) regularly ['rɛgjələ·li] adv. 定期地

(2) February ['februərɪ] n. 二月

(3) particularly [pə'tɪkjʊləlɪ] adv. 特别地

(4) hereditary [hɪredɪt(ə)rɪ] adj. 遗传的

(5) prioritising [praɪ'ɒrɪtaɪzɪŋ] v. 优先处理

(6) pronunciation [prə,nʌnsɪ'eɪʃ(ə)n] n. 发音

(7) prejudice ['predʒʊdɪs] n. 偏见

(8) facilitate [fə'sɪlɪteɪt] v. 促进

(9) hospitable [hɒ'spɪtəb(ə)l] adj. 热情友好的

(10) onomatopoeia [ɒnə(ʊ)mætə'piːə] n. 拟声

2. Read the words

(1) rice—race	(5) load—lord	(9) stared—starred
(2) tile—tale	(6) find—found	(10) coat—caught
(3) lime—lamb	(7) shout—shot	(11) lock—lord—look
(4) row—raw	(8) vary—very	(12) beat—bet—bet—bat

3. Read the phrases

(1) Friday flight	(5) a period of fear	(9) a hairy bear
(2) a broken bowl	(6) hear the cheers	(10) the curious jury
(3) a blue balloon	(7) a fair in the square	(11) fewer poor tourists
(4) sincere tears	(8) take care of the affair	(12) held his head high

4. Tongue Twist

(1) They knocked at the locked door loudly.

(2) He rarely read literary works.

(3) Equal pay for equal work.

(4) She sells shells on the seashore. The shells she sells are surely seashells. She's sure she sells seashore shells.

(5) How many cookies could a good cook cook if a good cook could cook cookies?

✨ VII. Note-taking Practice

Exercise 7: Listen and Copy [1]

1. What's the color of your new dress?

_____

2. What's the size of your shoes?

_____

3. How wide is this bridge?

_____

4. How thick is the ice here?

_____

5. This metal is harder than that one.

_____

6. He can run as fast as Jim.

_____

7. How often do you go swimming?

_____

8. This river is one third as long as that river.

_____

---

1 闫先凤 编：《听力密码：听见英国》，中国水利水电出版社，2019 年：第 52 页

Exercise 8: Listen and Write [1]

1. _____

2. _____

3. _____

4. _____

5. _____

6. _____

7. _____

8. _____

❧ VIII. Target Training

Exercise 9 [2]

A. Listen to the conversation about buying train tickets and choose the best choice.

1. What type of the ticket does the passenger buy?

(A) Saver Return   (B) Super Saver

(C) Standard Open Return   (D) First Open Return

2. How much is the ticket?

(A) £7.20   (B) £17.20

(C) £20.20   (D) £27.20

3. How does the passenger pay for the ticket?

(A) By cash   (B) By credit card

(C) By travellers cheque   (D) Not stated in the conversation

4. What time will the passenger arrive in Cambridge?

(A) 11:15   (B) 11:52

(C) 13:01   (D) 13:52

1　闫先凤 编：《听力密码：听见英国》，中国水利水电出版社，2019 年：第 49 页

2　上田真理砂 & Iain Davey 著，葛窈君 译：《听见英国——英式英语实境听力练习》，众文图书公司，2021 年：第 6 页

5. What will the passenger have to do at Kings Cross?

(A) Leave the station

(B) Change trains

(C) Go to Platform 13

(D) Not stated in the conversation

Tips[1]

英国车票的计费方式比中国的复杂许多，随着出发地、出发时间、出发日期、乘车路线不同，车票的名称和费用也跟着不同。

比如 Saver Return（来回票，价格比单程分开购买便宜），使用期限是一个月，而且视目的地不同，会限制星期一到星期五不能搭乘上午九点三十分之前的班车；Super Saver 周六和周日都不能使用；Standard Open Return 是出发时间不限、一个月内有效的来回票；First Open Return 是可以搭乘头等车厢（first class）、出发时间不限的一个月有效的来回票。

B. Listen to the conversation about *booking theatre tickets* and choose the best choice.[2]

Theatre Royal Drury Lane

Day to be booked	1. _____
Number of seats	2. _____
Type of show	Matinee / Evening show
Type of seats	● Balcony
	● 3. _____
	● Dress Circle
	● Stalls
	● Box Seats
Method of payment	4. _____
Total price of tickets	5. _____
Number of seats	6. _____

1　上田真理砂 & Iain Davey 著，葛窈君 译：《听见英国——英式英语实境听力练习》，众文图书公司，2021 年：第 4 页

2　上田真理砂 & Iain Davey 著，葛窈君 译：《听见英国——英式英语实境听力练习》，众文图书公司，2021 年：第 50 页

Tips

伦敦的 Covent Garden（科芬园）是音乐剧、歌剧、芭蕾等表演活动的圣地，不同种类的座位有不同票价，而每个剧场又各有不同的座位名称，可以利用网络事先查询座位的名称和价格，也可以在网络上直接订票。通常 balcony 的座位最便宜，box seat 最贵。

Matinee（日场，包括音乐剧、歌剧、芭蕾等表演）通常在星期三和星期六的日间上演，价格比较便宜，可以穿着轻便的服装前往观赏。

Exercise 10: Write the Numbers in the News [1]

1. Mars rover travels over _____ meters

China's Mars rover Zhurong traveled more than _____ meters on the surface of the red planet as of 11 pm Saturday, according to the Lunar Exploration and Space Program Center of the China National Space Administration. The rover will soon arrive at the _____ sand dune on its journey on the red planet. It will carry out a detailed survey of the dune and surrounding environment, said the administration. As of Saturday, Zhurong had been operating on the surface of Mars for _____ Martian days. A Martian day is approximately _____ longer than a day on Earth. About _____ away from Earth, the orbiter of Tianwen-1 had operated in orbit for _____ days as of Saturday. The delay of its one-way communication was around _____. Both the Mars rover Zhurong and Tianwen-1 spacecraft are working in normal conditions, with their subsystems operating normally, according to the administration.

2. Incredible list of inventory shipped to Japan

A _____ horses, _____ sofas, _____ tea bags and a red telephone box barely scrape the surface of the inventory that the British Olympic Association have shipped to Japan for this summer's delayed Tokyo Games. Barring any late hiccups, _____ Team GB athletes will compete in Tokyo, the largest number at any Games on foreign soil since the _____ went to Spain _____ years ago. They will also be accompanied by _____ coaches and other support staff. "One of the big differences this time is the amount of Covid mitigation supplies, including face masks, PPE(个人防护用品), sanitizer and some specialist equipment such as self-

---

1　https://baijiahao.baidu.com/s?id=1705796473508546450&wfr=spider&for=pc

sanitizing button covers for lifts," says Mark England, of the British Olympic Association.

3. Global economy to grow by _____

The International Monetary Fund(IMF，国际货币基金组织) on Tuesday maintained its global economic growth forecast at _____ for _____, with economic prospects diverging further across countries since April's forecast, according to the latest World Economic Outlook (WEO). According to the latest projection, growth prospects for advanced economies this year have improved by _____ percentage points to reach _____, while those for emerging market and developing economies this year are downgraded by _____ percentage points to _____. Close to _____ of the population in advanced economies are fully vaccinated, compared with _____ in emerging market economies, and a tiny fraction in low-income developing countries, IMF Chief Economist Gita Gopinath said at a virtual press briefing.

4. UN report warns of 'dramatic worsening' of hunger

The year _____ saw a dramatic worsening of world hunger, which affected an estimated _____ to _____ people, the United Nations Food and Agriculture Organization said in a statement on Monday. The warning came with the launch of "The State of Food Security and Nutrition in the World _____" . The report, drafted by the FAO in cooperation with other four UN agencies, urged the global community to act swiftly to help the world get back on track to reach Goal _____ of the Sustainable Development Agenda, which is to end hunger and malnutrition by _____.

Last year, global hunger grew in both absolute and proportional terms, outpacing the population growth. "Some _____ of all people are estimated to have been undernourished last year, up from _____ in _____," the report said. If current trends are maintained, the UN agencies estimated Goal _____ would be missed "by a margin of nearly _____ people."

Further data showed children remained the most exposed in the pandemic year, as more than _____ of those aged under _____ were estimated to have been stunted, another _____ too thin, and nearly _____ overweight.

🎐 IX. Listen and Understand the Culture

Exercise 11: Listen, Read and Speak

A Guide to British Etiquette [1]
英国礼仪

"The customary code of polite behaviour in society or among members of a particular profession or group." —Etiquette, the Oxford English Dictionary definition. Every culture across the ages has been defined by the concept of etiquette and accepted social interaction. However, it is the British—and the English in particular—who have historically been known to place a great deal of importance in good manners.

"礼貌行为习惯存在于社会或特定职业或群体中"，这是牛津英语词典对礼仪下的定义。对礼仪和公认社交的看法定义了不同时代的每种文化。然而，就是英国人，特别是英格兰人，他们有史以来一直以非常注重儒雅的行为而闻名。

When meeting someone for the first time a handshake is always preferable to a hug and a kiss on the cheek is reserved for close friends only. Asking personal questions about salary, relationship status, weight or age (particularly in the case of more 'mature' ladies) is also frowned upon.

初次见面握手常常要比拥抱更可取，亲吻面颊仅仅是留给亲密朋友的。询问个人有关工资、情感状况、体重或者年龄问题（特别是对于比较成熟的女士来说）也是不提倡的。

Should you be invited to a British dinner party it is customary for a dinner guest to bring a gift for the host or hostess, such as a bottle of wine, a bouquet of flowers or chocolates. Good table manners are essential and unless you are attending a barbeque or an informal buffet it is frowned upon to use fingers rather than cutlery to eat. The cutlery should also be held correctly, i.e. the knife in the right hand and the fork in the left hand. At a formal dinner party when there are numerous utensils at your place setting it is customary to begin with the utensils on the outside.

---

1 闫先凤 编：《听力密码：听见英国》，中国水利水电出版社，2019 年：第 170 页

如果你被邀请参加一个英国的晚宴，赴晚宴的人按照习俗应当为男主人或女主人带礼物，如一瓶葡萄酒、一束鲜花或一份巧克力。良好的餐桌举止是必不可少的，除非你参加一个烧烤或非正式的自助餐，否则用手指而不是用餐具用餐是令人生厌的。持拿餐具的方式也应当正确，即左手拿叉、右手拿刀。在一个正式的宴会上，你的左右有很多餐具，习惯的做法是从外部开始取用餐具。

As the guest it is polite to wait until everyone at the table has been served and your host starts eating or indicates that you should do so. Once the meal has begun it is impolite to reach over someone else's plate for an item such as seasoning or a food platter; it is more considerate to ask for the item to be passed to you. Leaning your elbows on the table whilst you are eating is also considered rude.

作为客人，等待餐桌旁所有人用餐，等待主人开始用餐，或者说你应该这样做，这才是有礼貌的。一旦就餐开始，越过他人的盘子拿取物品是不礼貌的，例如调味品或是餐盘；而请人将物品传递给你则是得体的行为。边吃饭边把你的胳膊肘支在桌子上，也被认为是粗鲁的。

Slurping or making other such loud noises whilst eating is completely frowned upon. As with yawning or coughing it is also considered very rude to chew open-mouthed or talk when there is still food in your mouth. These actions imply that a person was not brought up to adhere to good manners, a criticism against not only the offender but their family too!

吃饭时出声是绝对禁止的。正如吃饭时打呵欠或咳嗽一样，食物在你的嘴里而你边咀嚼边说话也被认为是非常粗鲁的。这些行为表明，一个人如果没有从小学会遵循良好的举止，该遭到谴责的不仅是行为不当的人，而且还有他们的家人！

More recently, a rise in multiculturalism, a changing economy and the introduction of social and gender specific equality laws have all played a part in Britain moving away from its rigid class system of old, and therefore a more informal attitude to social etiquette has arisen. However, today Britain has been influenced by the importance of corporate etiquette, with a shift in focus from the social or household setting to an emphasis on business etiquette and protocol. Indeed, the rise in online business and social media sites has even seen the creation of a worldwide "online society", necessitating its own rules of conduct, commonly referred to as Netiquette, or network etiquette. These rules regarding the protocol for such communications as email, forums and blogs are constantly being redefined as the internet continues to evolve.

近来，多元文化的兴起、经济状况的波动及相关社会平等和性别平等法律的出台都使英国摆脱了僵化的贵族制度的束缚，因此人们对社会礼仪的态度也更加随心所欲了。然而，现如今，英国也受到企业礼仪的重大影响，而从注重社会或家庭礼仪转向了商务礼仪和外交礼仪。事实上，随着电子商务和社交媒体网站的兴起，一个世界范围的"网络社会"也产生了，因此网络行为规则应运而生，通常称为网络礼仪。这些涉及像电子邮件、论坛和博客中的礼仪规则随着互联网的持续发展常常被重新定义。

What have you learnt from this passage?

1. New words

_____

_____

2. Summary

_____

_____

3. Your opinion

_____

_____

Game Time—Sudoku

● How to play the game

The goal of Sudoku is to fill in a 9 × 9 grid with digits so that each column, row, and 3 × 3 section contain the numbers between 1 and 9. At the beginning of the game, the 9 × 9 grid will have some of the squares filled in. Your job is to use logic to fill in the missing digits and complete the grid. Don't forget, a move is incorrect if:

- Any row contains more than one of the same number from 1 to 9

- Any column contains more than one of the same number from 1 to 9

- Any 3 × 3 grid contains more than one of the same number from 1 to 9

● Sudoku Tips

Sudoku is a fun puzzle game once you get the hang of it. At the same time, learning to play Sudoku can be a bit intimidating for beginners. So, if you are a complete beginner, here are a few Sudoku tips that you can use to improve your Sudoku skills.

Tip 1: Look for rows, columns of 3 × 3 sections that contain 5 or more numbers. Work through the remaining empty cells, trying the numbers that have not been used. In many cases, you will find numbers that can only be placed in one position considering the other numbers that are already in its row, column, and 3 × 3 grid.

Tip 2: Break the grid up visually into 3 columns and 3 rows. Each large column will have 3, 3 × 3 grids and each row will have 3, 3 × 3 grids. Now, look for columns or grids that have 2 of the same number. Logically, there must be a 3rd copy of the same number in the only remaining 9-cell section. Look at each of the remaining 9 positions and see if you can find the location of the missing number.

Unit 3

Time and Date

Objectives:

● to know the expression of time, date and year

● to learn about the date of birth of some famous musicians

● to learn about calendar and leap year

● to know the listening skill—understanding the differences between American English and British English

● to know the Greenwich Standard Time

 **I. Warm up**

Exercise 1: Dictation of Words

1. _____   6. _____   11. _____   16. _____

2. _____   7. _____   12. _____   17. _____

3. _____   8. _____   13. _____   18. _____

4. _____   9. _____   14. _____   19. _____

5. _____   10. _____   15. _____   20. _____

II. Background Information [1]

Part I Time

1. 整点:

例如: 现在是两点整。

- It's two.
- It's two o'clock.
- It's two o'clock **sharp**.
- It's two o'clock **on the dot**.
- It's two o'clock **on the nose**.
- It's **exactly** two o'clock.

另外，英语中的 noon 和 midnight 可分别直接表示白天和夜晚的 12 点:

- It's (twelve) noon. 现在是中午十二点。
- It's (twelve) midnight. 现在是半夜零点。

2. 几点几分

（1）直接表达法: 用基数词按钟点＋分钟的顺序直接写出时间。如:

| 11:05 eleven o-five | 8:30 eight thirty |
| 7:40 seven forty | 2:43 two forty-three |

（2）间接表达法:

- 如果所表述的时间超出半小时，可以用 "分钟＋past＋小时"

6:10 ten past six   4:20 twenty past four   10:25 twenty-five past ten

- 如果所表述的时间在半小时之内，可以用 "（相差的）分钟+to+（下一）小时"

10:35 twenty-five to eleven   5:50 ten to six

（3）特殊时间点: two to two, nine three quarters, half past three

3. 上下午

- 12 小时制: am/ a.m. / AM, pm/ p.m. / PM, 比如 7:30 a.m., 7:30 p.m.
- 24 小时制: 没有 am 或 pm, 比如 13:00 pm, 这种就是错误写法

---

1 https://j.51tietu.net/juzi/1515075.html

4. 特殊时间

midmorning, midday, midnight, midsummer, mid-autumn

5. 英语美语在时、分表达上的差异

➢ 表示几点差几分时英语用"to"，而美语用"before"或"of"，如"10 点 50 分"可以说成：ten to eleven（英语）或 ten before（或 of）eleven（美语）

➢ 表示几点过几分时英语用"past"，而美语用 after 如"11 点 10 分"可以说成：ten past eleven（英语）或 ten after eleven（美语）

➢ 在表示时刻缩写形式的数字中英语多用句号，而美语多用冒号，如：6.30（英语），或 6：30（美语）

➢ 表示"半小时"的差异：half an hour（英语），或 a half hour（美语）

Part II Days

Spelling Exercise 1: Write down the Days in English

周一	周二	周三
周四	周五	周六
周日	工作日	周末
14 天 / 两周	休息天	国定假日

Part III Dates

1. 在英式英语中，通常可有两种表达法，即（以"1988 年 5 月 2 日"为例）：

（1）写法：(the) 2(nd) May, 1988

读法：the second of May, nineteen eighty-eight（of 要读出来，但不用写出来）

（2）写法：May (the) 2(nd), 1988

读法：May the second, nineteen eighty-eight

2. 在美式英语中，通常只采用一种表达法，即（以"1988 年 5 月 2 日"为例）：

写法：May 2(nd), 1988

读法：May second, nineteen eighty-eight

注意，写法中：

➢ 日期与月份之间不可以加逗号。

➢ 年份前的逗号可以省略。

➢ 代表日期的序数词词尾（-st，-nd，-rd 或 -th）均可省略。

➤ 序数词前的定冠词 the，一般可省略（尤其是以序数词开头的场合）；但在读法中，英式英语该定冠词则不省略，而美式英语该定冠词一般也省略。

Spelling Exercise 2: Write down the Dates

1. 11 月 24 日		7. 1 月 31 日	
2. 6 月 20 日		8. 12 月 2 日	
3. 9 月 22 日		9. 3 月 11 日	
4. 10 月 28 日		10. 5 月 5 日	
5. 7 月 26 日		11. 8 月 12 日	
6. 2 月 2 日		12. 4 月 23 日	

Spelling Exercise 3: Fill in the Form

月份	English	Abbreviation	Special expression	Festival
1 月			The first month	New Year's Day
2 月				Valentine's Day
3 月				
4 月				April Fool's Day/Easter Day
5 月				Mother's Day
6 月				Father's Day
7 月				
8 月				Summer Bank Holiday
9 月				
10 月				Halloween
11 月				Thanksgiving Day
12 月			The last month	Christmas Day

Part IV　Years and Ages

1. era 年代，时代　　6. decade 十年　　　　　　11. modern times 近代 = contemporary

2. epoch 纪元　　　　7. score years 二十年　　12. Ice Age 冰河世纪

3. age 时期，年龄　　8. a quarter century 二十五年　　13. Renaissance 文艺复兴时期

4. period 时期，阶段　9. half a century 五十年　　14. Neolithic Age 新时期时代

5. century 世纪　　　10. ancient times 古代　　15. Medieval 中古世纪

in the 1980s = in the 1980's = in the 80's

in the early 1980s, in the mid-1980s, in the late 20th century

Part V Prepositions Before Time

in	after	not... until	over
on	before	for	since
at	until/till	during	from... to/between... and

III. Testing Key Points

1. 出生日期
2. 约见时间
3. 上课时间
4. 开门时间、关门时间、营业时长
5. 成立时间、发展状况
6. 租赁时间，居住时长，入住时间
7. 工作时间：上班，加班，轮休等
8. 联系时间
9. 面试时间
10. 订单完成时间
11. 活动时间
12. 车程远近
13. 借书还书
14. 使用时长
15. 频率次数
16. 参观时长，集合时间
17. 出版时间

IV. Word Bank

1. date of birth 出生日期
2. meeting time 会议时间
3. opening time 营业时间
4. close time 关门时间
5. founded/established/set up in 成立于
6. rent from 从……租
7. length of stay 停留时间
8. move in on 在哪天搬进去
9. time off 休假，放假
10. overwork/work overtime 加班
11. day/night/two shifts 早晚班
12. contact time/time for message 联系时间
13. order within... days 订单在……天内
14. two-hour drive/5-minute walk 2小时车程 / 5分钟步行
15. due time/overdue 过期的，延误的
16. keep the book for 借书（多长时间）
17. every other week/every two weeks 每两周
18. time for visit 访问时间
19. published after 2000 2000年后出版
20. three consecutive days 连续3天
21. at midday 在正午
22. fortnight 两星期

✿ V. Basic Training [1]

Exercise 2: Write down What You Hear

A. Times

1.   2.   3.   4.   5.

B. Days

1.   2.   3.   4.   5.

C. Years

1.   2.   3.   4.   5.   6.

Exercise 3

Are these times the same or different from those on the tape? Mark the correct ones with "√"

and the wrong ones with "×".

| 1. 12:15 | 2. 2:35 | 3. 4:45 | 4. 9:30 | 5. 9:15 |
| 6. 1:20 | 7. 1:45 | 8. 11:05 | 9. 4:00 | 10. 9:40 |

Exercise 4

Listen to the tape and complete the following statements.

1. Dr. Blake wasn't born until _____.

2. I'll see you at _____.

3. She doesn't live in _____ Street.

4. You weren't with us on _____.

5. I'd like to phone _____, that's _____. _____.

6. Mrs. Jones has an appointment at _____.

7. A northeast wind will bring rain to the _____ area _____.

---

1   https://www.tingclass.net/show-6697-114768-1.html

Exercise 5 [1]

A. Listen to the tape. Write T if the statement is true and write F if the statement is false.

1. The cinema is open every day.

2. Weekday ticket prices are cheaper than weekend ones.

3. The information is for Friday through Thursday.

4. *Men in Black II* is on every weekday.

5. *Triple X*'s first show is at 12:20, from Monday to Wednesday.

B. Listen to the tape again and choose the best answer.

1. What cinema is this information line for?

A. Odeon Kensington

B. Leicester

C. Odeon Square

D. Odeon Leicester Square

2. What is the price range of weekday tickets?

A. £5 to £6.5

B. £5 to £10

C. £6 to £11

D. £10 to £11

3. Which film(s) can be seen at the weekend?

A. *Harry Potter*

B. *Harry Potter* and *Triple X*

C. *Men in Black II*

D. *Men in Black II* and *Minority Report*

4. Which day(s) is there a late show?

A. Thursday

B. Friday

C. Friday and Saturday

D. Saturday and Sunday

5. When is the Minority Report?

A. Monday 12:20 pm

B. At the weekend

C. After *Men in Black II*

D. Friday at 12:10

---

1 上田真理砂 & Iain Davey 著，葛窈君 译：《听见英国——英式英语实境听力练习》，众文图书公司，2021 年：第 52 页

VI. Listening Skill 3—British English and American English [1]

1. 拼写

一般而言，美式英语的拼写比英式英语更接近发音，这是美式英语的特征。对已经熟悉和习惯美式英语的读者来说，可能多少会觉得英式拼法有些不习惯。以下就美式和英式英语拼写的不同，举出几个具体例子加以说明。请注意，虽然看起来变化相当规则，但是例外也不少，不是所有的单词变化都可以套上公式。

例 1   -tre

theatre	theater	(n.) 剧场
centre	center	(n.) 中心
litre	liter	(n.) 公升

美式英语中以 -ter 结尾的单词，基本上在英式英语中会变成 -tre，例外的情形如 porter（搬运工人）、carpenter（木匠），美式英语拼法与英式英语相同。

例 2   -our

colour	color	(n.) 颜色
neighbour	neighbor	(n.) 邻居
rumour	rumor	(n.) 谣言

美式英语中以 -or 结尾的单词，基本上在英式英语中会变成 -our，例外的情况如 visitor，monitor，美式英语拼写与英式英语相同。

例 3   -logue

dialogue	dialog	(n.) 对话
catalogue	catalog	(n.) 目录

美式英语中以 -log 结尾的单词，基本上在英式英语中会变成 -logue。

例 4   -gue/que-

cheque	check	(n.) 支票
queue	cue	(n.) 排队

美式英语的拼法原本与英式英语一样，后来为了贴近发音而改变拼写方式。

---

1   上田真理砂 & Iain Davey 著，葛窈君 译：《听见英国——英式英语实境听力练习》，众文图书公司，2021 年：第 18 页

例 5   -ll/-l

travelling	traveling	(a) 旅行的
fulfil	fulfill	(v.) 执行

美式英语中有些是 -l- 的单词，在英式英语中会变成 -ll-，相反的情形也有，有些在美式英语中是 -ll- 的单词，在英式英语中会变成 -l-。

例 6   -mme

programme	program	(n.) 节目
kilogramme	kilogram	(n.) 公斤

美式英语中以 -m 结尾单词，有些在英式英语中会变成 -mme，例外的情况如 poem（诗）、stadium（体育场），美式英语拼法与英式英语相同。

例 7   -se

organise	organize	(v.) 组织
realise	realize	(v.) 领悟

美式英语中以 -ze 结尾的单词，基本上在英式英语中会变成 -se。例外的情形如 gaze（凝视）、gauze（纱布），美式英语拼法与英式英语相同。

例 8   -ce

licence (n.)	license (n./v.)	执照；批准
license (v.)		
practice (n.)	practice (n./v.)	实行；练习
practise (v.)		
defence (n.)	defense (n.)	防御；抵抗

美式英语中以 -se 结尾的单词，基本上名词和动词的拼法相同，但在英式英语中名词是 -ce，动词是 -se。

2. 发音

<table>
<tr><td colspan="6" align="center">表 1 英式英语的元音</td></tr>
<tr><td></td><td>例</td><td>IPA</td><td></td><td>例</td><td>IPA</td></tr>
<tr><td>1</td><td>bead</td><td>i:</td><td>11</td><td>bought</td><td>ɔ:</td></tr>
<tr><td>2</td><td>bit</td><td>i</td><td>12</td><td>kite</td><td>ai</td></tr>
<tr><td>3</td><td>date</td><td>ei</td><td>13</td><td>bout</td><td>au</td></tr>
<tr><td>4</td><td>bed</td><td>e</td><td>14</td><td>boil</td><td>ɔi</td></tr>
<tr><td>5</td><td>bath</td><td>a:</td><td>15</td><td>bird</td><td>ɜ:</td></tr>
<tr><td>6</td><td>sat</td><td>æ</td><td>16</td><td>bottom</td><td>ə</td></tr>
<tr><td>7</td><td>food</td><td>u:</td><td>17</td><td>lock</td><td>ɔ</td></tr>
<tr><td>8</td><td>foot</td><td>u</td><td>18</td><td>beard</td><td>iə</td></tr>
<tr><td>9</td><td>boat</td><td>əu</td><td>19</td><td>scare</td><td>eə</td></tr>
<tr><td>10</td><td>fun</td><td>ʌ</td><td>20</td><td>gourd</td><td>uə</td></tr>
</table>

<table>
<tr><td colspan="6" align="center">表 2 美式英语的元音</td></tr>
<tr><td></td><td>例</td><td>IPA</td><td></td><td>例</td><td>IPA</td></tr>
<tr><td>1</td><td>bead</td><td>i:</td><td>11</td><td>bought</td><td>ɔ:</td></tr>
<tr><td>2</td><td>bit</td><td>i</td><td>12</td><td>kite</td><td>ai</td></tr>
<tr><td>3</td><td>date</td><td>ei</td><td>13</td><td>bout</td><td>au</td></tr>
<tr><td>4</td><td>bed</td><td>e</td><td>14</td><td>boil</td><td>ɔi</td></tr>
<tr><td>5</td><td>bath</td><td>a:</td><td>15</td><td>bird</td><td>ɜ:</td></tr>
<tr><td>6</td><td>sat</td><td>æ</td><td>16</td><td>bottom</td><td>ə</td></tr>
<tr><td>7</td><td>food</td><td>u:</td><td>17</td><td>lock</td><td>ɑ:</td></tr>
<tr><td>8</td><td>foot</td><td>u</td><td>18</td><td>beard</td><td>ir</td></tr>
<tr><td>9</td><td>boat</td><td>ou</td><td>19</td><td>scare</td><td>er</td></tr>
<tr><td>10</td><td>fun</td><td>ʌ</td><td>20</td><td>gourd</td><td>ʊr</td></tr>
</table>

例 1　[f, θ, s, m, n] 前的元音

| path | [pɑ:θ] | [pæθ] | (n.) 小路 |
| dance | [dɑ:ns] | [dæns] | (v.) 跳舞 |

在 [辅音 + a + 辅音] 的音节中，[f, θ, s, m, n] 前的元音在美式英语发成 [æ]，在英式英语则发成 [a:]。

| pass | [pɑ:s] | [pæs] | (v.) 通过 |
| laugh | [lɑ:f] | [læf] | (v.) 笑 |

美式英语中如 pass, laugh 等单词中的元音 [æ] 一般发成短音，但英式英语则发成长音 [a:]。

例 2　双元音

| know | [nəʊ] | [noʊ] | (v.) 知道 |

美式英语中的 [oʊ] 音，在英式英语中发成 [əʊ]。

例 3　单元音

| can't | [ka:nt] | [kænt] | (aux.) 无法 |

can 这个词不论在美式或英式英语中，都可以用发音的强弱表达不同语气，表示强调的时候发成 [kæn]，没有特别强调时发成 [kən]。另外，美式英语比英式英语更常使用 [ə] 这个音，英式英语则比较常用 [a:] 这个音。

| top | [tɒp] | [tɑp] | (n.) 顶部 |
| hot | [hɒt] | [hɑt] | (a.) 热的 |

美式英语中如 top, hot 等单词的元音发 [a] 音，在英式英语中则是发成 [ɔ]。

| hiccup/hiccough | [ˈhɪkəp] | [ˈhɪkʌp] | (n.) 打嗝 |
| uphold | [əpˈhəʊld] | [ʌpˈhoʊld] | (v.) 举起 |

hiccup, uphold 等单词中的元音 [ʌ]，如果不是特别强调，一般念成 [ə]。

例 4　元音后的 /r/

| water | [ˈwɔːtə(r)] | [ˈwɔːtər] | (n.) 水 |
| bitter | [ˈbɪtə(r)] | [ˈbɪtər] | (a.) 苦的 |

同英式英语相比，美式英语单词结尾的 [r] 发音比较重。美式英语中 [t] 的发音比较接近 [d]，发音并不是很清楚。此外，美式英语有个很大的特征，元音中间的 [t] 会发成类似 [d] 的弹舌音。另外，英式英语不发出单词结尾的 [r] 音，而 [t] 的发音则比较清晰。

例 5　wh-

| which | [wɪtʃ] | [wen] | (pron.) 哪一个 |
| when | [hwɪtʃ] | [hwen] | (adv.) 什么时候 |

以 wh 开头的单词，在美式英语的发音中会在 [w] 之前加上一点 [h] 的音，相对地，英式英语则不发 [h] 的音，直接发 [w] 的音。因此，英式英语中 which 和 witch 发音相同。

例 6　以 -ile 结尾的单词

| fragile | [ˈfrædʒaɪl] | [ˈfrædʒl] | adj. 易碎的；易损的 |
| hostile | [ˈhɒstaɪl] | [ˈhɑːstl] | adj. 敌意的；敌对的 |

以 -ile 结尾的单词，在英式英语中发 [ai] 音，美式英语中一般不发 [ai] 音。

3. 语调

这里所说的语调，不是指声音的强弱，而是指特定的发音或说话方式。从语调可以了解关于说话者的一些事情，比如出生地、社会阶级、教育水平、这种语言是不是说话者的母语等。美国并没有什么社会阶级的观念，但英国现在对社会阶级的看法仍然根深蒂固地受到传统观念的影响。

美国虽然没有什么社会阶级观念，但从说话者使用的语法或服装仍然可以大致推测其教育水平。相对地，英式英语说话者的语调比美式英语可以看出更多含义，尤其是政治家，在重要演说前接受所谓 elocution lesson（演说课）发音矫正指导的例子十分常见。最有名的当属撒切尔夫人（英国首位女性首相，在任期间：1975—1990 年），为了刻意压低声音，甚至请语音专家来指导。这是因为一般在英国，低音会比高音更能给人信任感，可以增加信赖度。此外，电视或电台主播及播报员、舞台演员等从事与声音相关工作的人员，接受发音矫正指导的例子也很常见。

✿ VII. Note-taking Practice

Exercise 6: Listen and Copy [1]

1. It's ten minutes to four.

_____

2. It's not four o'clock.

_____

3. My watch is two minutes fast.

_____

4. We must arrive there on time.

_____

5. There are only two minutes left.

_____

6. Can you finish your work ahead of time?

_____

7. The flight is delayed.

_____

8. The meeting is put off.

_____

1　闫先凤 编：《听力密码：听见英国》，中国水利水电出版社，2019 年：第 47 页

Exercise 7: Listen and Write the Key Information of Time in the Train Announcements [1]

1. _____

2. _____

3. _____

4. _____

5. _____

6. _____

7. _____

8. _____

9. _____

10. _____

VIII. Target Training

Exercise 8 [2]

You will hear the dates of birth and the dates of death of ten world famous composers. Listen carefully. Fill in the blanks with the dates you hear. Write as rapidly as you can. You may use short forms for the months. For example, Jan. for January; Feb. for February.

1. Johann Bach, a famous German composer, was born on _____ and died on _____.

2. George Handel, a well-known German-born British composer, was born on _____ and died on _____.

3. Wolfgang Mozart was a brilliant Austrian composer, who was born on _____ and died on _____.

4. Ludwig van Beethoven, an ingenious German composer, was born on_____ and died on _____.

5. As one of the outstanding Austrian composers, Franz Schubert was born on _____ and died on _____.

---

1 上田真理砂 & Iain Davey 著，葛窈君 译：《听见英国 英式英语实境听力练习》，众文图书公司，2021 年：第 212 页

2 http://www.kekenet.com/Article/200906/75959.shtml

6. Felix Mendelssohn, another famous German composer, was born on _____ and died on _____.

7. Poland also produced a well-known composer, Frederic Chopin, who was born on _____ and died on _____.

8. Franz Liszt was a renowned Hungarian composer. He was born on _____ and died on _____.

9. Johann Strauss, another celebrated Austrian composer, was born on _____ and died on _____.

10. As the most prominent Russian composer, Peter Tchaikovsky was born on _____ and died on _____.

Exercise 9: They're All on Calendars [1]

Listen to the passage and complete the sentences below.

1. The New Year is the time for _____. It is also the time to buy a new _____.

2. There are lots and lots of choices, small, big, the one that sits on a _____ that hang on _____. Calendars to carry around. Calendars that show a whole _____ or one day at a time.

3. All calendars are the same. They all list the same days of the year in exactly the same _____. Calendars have become popular _____ because many are filled with beautiful pictures.

4. Some have pictures of famous _____. They often give information about their _____— such as famous _____ or American Indians or flower gardens.

5. There are some calendars about _____, places, sports and _____, and others with popular cartoon characters and famous people, like Elvis Presley or Marilyn Monroe.

6. For pet lovers, there are calendars with pictures of _____ doing unusual things. Calendars of dogs wearing _____. And calendars of beautiful women in _____.

7. There are calendars with _____, too. There are even calendars for _____ who can draw the pictures themselves.

8. Some people use calendars to write down important things they must remember, like _____ or doctor's appointments.

1　https://www.tingclass.net/show-8394-269704-1.html

9. But what if they forget to look at their calendar? Do not worry, there are _____ organizers that make _____ to remind people of things they must do.

10. Some people are happy just to write down _____ to themselves on small pieces of paper.

Exercise 10: Summary [1]

Listen to the passages and complete the blanks.

Passage A: Leap Year（闰年）

The reason for a leap day or a leap year is because our calendar does not follow the Earth's _____ around the sun exactly. So every _____ years, we put all that time together into an _____ day—or, what is officially called an intercalary day — "Leap day".

"Leap" is also an important word for two other common— but _____ —American expressions. One is a kind of _____— "Look before you leap." The other expression is a phrase of _____ —to "take a leap of faith" invites the person to take action. Interestingly, both phrases are completely reasonable to say to someone who is about to get _____.

Passage B: Phases in Life（人生的阶段）[2]

A change of seasons will be like this, daylight grow shorter, and _____ drop. Plants stop producing _____. Leaves change _____. Some animals become less active and _____ during the winter months.

Nature has its phases and so do we. Spring is a time of _____, like the time when we enter the world as innocent as a newborn baby. Then babies become _____. Bad behavior can be a

---

1 https://www.baidu.com/link?url=0xEXkwCQzc511vmEmy1wzL-Uvj4LZTr2g_UVSQkFjIkUkMFj-yz7WoMX7936GulfL--8MS-I1Dxqx9e6dKUSlwYHQkb3w7HcOGrMoff08GKolyWE5qcYCKVDsSxXcv-w&wd=&eqid=a705efb90000cb0f0000000363eaf7a6

2 https://www.baidu.com/link?url=Rz6ESirq6WpbLDQ4BJtLkYc_dWvlUHIHJu3RW51XO6v9_LZV3rZH6K4NOWs8m6BBkPjs3CLHudS2sGNpBGN-Q1x6r0Mim4qpy-5buozBzRQYx9NkWlPGz_pqnjqv47Rj8MiWYAGYuybbdvc8QpTesK&wd=&eqid=a93e56840003034400000000263eaf825

problem during this period. But childhood is a _____ time, when everything seems possible. However, those feelings of wonder are often dampened during a child's _____. Then we become young adults.

20s and 30s are the _____ of life at one's personal best. Some people _____ really early, in high school or college. After that, it may be all _____. They will have memories of the _____ days—always reliving an earlier, happier time. Other people may be late _____.

Whenever you peak, we all begin to slow down a bit. As we age, we enter the _____, busy working and possibly raising a family. We may feel life predictable and have the _____. They may buy a really fast _____, get a tattoo or take up a new and dangerous hobby—like _____.

After that, we enter the next phase—the autumn years—the season of _____. Our autumn years is the period after we _____ from work and start to slow down. We have other terms called the _____ years, or better, the _____ years to describe a time that is _____ and easy. Some people in their autumn years of life may have some _____. But seriously, who wouldn't? Nearly everyone has a few "what-ifs" and "should-haves."

IX. Listen and Understand the Culture

Exercise 11: Listen, Read and Speak

Why Was Greenwich Standard Time Created? [1]
格林尼治标准时间

Imagine getting on a train at twelve noon and heading out on a four-hour trip to another town.

设想一下：你正乘坐一辆中午 12 点整出发的火车前往另外一个城市，途中预计花费 4 个小时。

---

1 闫先凤 编：《听力密码：听见英国》，中国水利水电出版社，2019 年：第 153 页

You'd expect to arrive at four o'clock in the afternoon, right? But before the last few decades of the 19th century, there was no guarantee that this would happen, and it usually had little to do with slow trains or drunken conductors.

你肯定期望在下午四点能够准时到达，对吧？但是，在19世纪中后期的几十年中，没人能保障火车一定准时准点，而且这与晚点或醉酒的列车长几乎毫无关系。

Until the end of the 19th century virtually every town across the world kept time according to its own methods, creating problems for industries such as railroads that relied on precise timing to deliver goods.

实际上直到19世纪末，几乎世界上每个城市都有自己的计时方式，这就给一些行业，如铁路运输业带来无尽的麻烦。因为铁路运输需要按准确时间发送货物。

To bring order to this chaos, a conference was held in Washington, D.C. in 1884. Delegates from around the world designated Greenwich England as the starting point from which to create an international time zone.

为了改变这种混乱局面，各国代表于1884年在华盛顿特区召开了一次会议。代表们指定英国格林尼治区作为创建国际时区的起点。

But why was this small, London suburb chosen to create what became known as Greenwich Standard Time?

为什么伦敦郊区这个小镇会被选为创建格林尼治标准时间呢？

Over 100 years before the Washington conference, King George II of England designated Greenwich as zero degrees longitude in order to help stabilize the shipping trade. If you look at a globe of the earth you'll see that the vertical line marked 'zero' that runs from the North to the South Pole-zero degrees longitude—runs directly through Greenwich.

在华盛顿会议100多年以前，英国国王乔治二世为了稳定航运业，曾将格林威治标为0度经线所在地。如果你看一下地球仪，你就会发现连接南北极的零度经线正好穿过格林尼治。

By the time of the Washington conference many shippers already used the longitude system to keep time when traveling by sea. It was only natural for most countries to adopt this system as the basis for creating standard time for the entire planet.

在华盛顿会议召开之时，许多航运公司在海运过程中已经使用经度系统来掌控时间。大多数国家自然就容易接受使用这一系统作为确认全球标准时间的基础。

Based on longitude increments of fifteen degrees, time becomes one hour earlier each longitude west of Greenwich, and one hour later each longitude east of Greenwich. In other words, when it's twelve noon at zero degrees longitude, it's one o'clock at fifteen longitude east.

以每增加经度 15 度为基准，格林尼治每往西 1 个时区时间便减少 1 个小时，而每往东 1 个时区则增加 1 个小时。换句话说，当零度经线处是中午 12 点时，东经 15 度处便是下午 1 点。

What have you learnt from this passage?

1. New words

_____

_____

_____

2. Summary

_____

_____

_____

3. Your opinion

_____

_____

_____

Places

Objectives:

- to know the components of spelling addresses
- to know the English names of some cities, countries and areas
- to know the places on and off campus
- to know the listening skills to deal with maps and plans
- to know further the differences between American English and British English

 **I. Warm up**

Exercise 1: Dictation of Words

1._____	6._____	11._____	16._____
2._____	7._____	12._____	17._____
3._____	8._____	13._____	18._____
4._____	9._____	14._____	19._____
5._____	10._____	15._____	20._____

II. Background Information

需要注意的是，在中国地址的表达方法是从大到小的顺序排列，但是西方国家地址表达方法往往<u>以从小到大</u>的顺序排列：house number and street name–town city-country state–postcode-country。

另外，英国的邮编是字母、数字组合成的，如：MK32KT。开头和结尾为字母，中间为数字。听的时候尤其注意 8 和 A 的区分，以及 C 和 6 的区分。

III. Testing Key Points

1. 房屋名称

● 一般都是考察一些常见的单词和短语，如 Sea View Guest House 和 International House。除此之外，还可能考到 flat, apartment 等。

2. 门牌号 + 街道名称 + 道路

● 门牌号就是一般的数字，而不是序数词，即是几而不是第几。

● 其次，街道名称有两种考法：

➤ 简单单词，如 forest, hill, park, garden, river, bank, north, south, central 等。这里面要尤其注意 forest 和 hill 两个单词，有必要区分 forest, first, fourth; hill, heel, heal, hell。山、河、森林会和 side 组在一起，例如 Hillside, Riverside, Woodside。同时注意 Woodside, ds 发生省音的现象，而且这三个单词都是合成词，不要分开写。

➤ 道路一般会考 6 个单词，分别为：road, street, avenue, lane, alley, drive。

● 常见的街道名称：Station Road, Market Street, Bank House, Gold Street, Park Square, Blossom Street, Earl Street, Circus Palace, Green Street, Park Street, Church Road, Lake Avenue, Fort Street。

3. 城市、国家和国籍

● 英联邦国家以及重要城市都是雅思听力里的考察点，这里涉及一些地理知识。但是，考题往往不会太难，题目里经常出现的国家有英国、美国、澳大利亚，日本和印度也会出现，频次稍微低一点，欧洲其他国家，比如德国、意大利、西班牙等出现的概率就更小了。

● 常考的城市名称见下面 Word Bank。

● 有些同学分不清楚国家和国籍，大家能记住 China 和 Chinese 的区别就应该明白了，写国籍的时候要写 Chinese，不能写 China。Word Bank 里列出了常考的国家和国籍，大家需要掌握这些词汇。

4. 校园内外的地点

● 校园内的地点往往与大学里的设施有关，教学设施比如阶梯教室、机房、图书馆等；生活设施比如食堂、寝室、洗衣房等；休闲娱乐设施比如健身房、游泳馆等。

● 校园外的设施就非常多了，衣食住行各行各业都有，数不胜数。

IV. Word Bank

1. Boroughs in London

Alton	Highbridge	Woodside
Hampshire	Greendale	Stamford
Canterbury	Westsea	Dumfries
Newton	Milperra	Docklands
South Hills	Bradfield	Grasford

2. City, County and Town

● **England**	● **Welsh**	Adelaide
London	Cardiff	Victoria
Liverpool	● **Northern Ireland**	Melbourne
Manchester	Belfast	Perth
Sheffield	● **Ireland**	● **New Zealand**
Birmingham	Dublin	Wellington
Coventry	● **Australia**	● **Canada**
Leeds	Canberra	Ottawa
● **Scotland**	Queensland	British Columbia
Edinburgh	Brisbane	Vancouver
Glasgow	Sydney	

3. Country and Nationality

Countries/Areas	Language	Nationality
America	English	American
Australia	English	Australian
Austria	Austrian	Austrian
Belgium	Belgian	Belgian
Britain	English	British
Canada	English	Canadian
China	Chinese	Chinese
Denmark	Danish	Danish
Egypt	Egyptian	Egyptian
France	French	French
Finland	Finnish	Finn
Germany	German	German
Greece	Greek	Greek
Hungary	Hungarian	Hungarian

Countries/Areas	Language	Nationality
India	Indian	Indian
Ireland	Irish	Irish
Italy	Italian	Italian
Japan	Japanese	Japanese
The Netherlands	Dutch	Dutch
New Zealand	English	New Zealander
Norway	Norwich	Norwich
Portugal	Portuguese	Portuguese
Russia	Russian	Russian
Scotland	Scottish	Scottish
Spain	Spanish	Spanish
Sweden	Swedish	Swedish
Switzerland	Swiss	Swiss
Wales	Welsh	Welsh

4. Continents and Oceans

Asia—Asian

Africa—African

Europe—European

North/South America—North/South American

Oceania—Oceanian

Antarctica—Antarctic

the Pacific Ocean

the Atlantic Ocean

the Indian Ocean

the Arctic Ocean

5. Places on Campus

（1）上课教室：

① Class 2 Grade 1

② PE Room

③ Science Lab

④ Robot Room

⑤ Art Room

⑥ Handwriting Room

⑦ Music Room

⑧ Dancing Hall

⑨ Computer Room

⑩ Special Edu Room

⑪ Amphitheatre

（2）办公室：

① Office for Grade 4

② Headmaster's Office

③ Vice Headmaster's Office

④ HR Office

⑤ Dean's Office

⑥ Edu R & D Office

⑦ English Office

⑧ Music Office

⑨ Art Office

⑩ Science Office

⑪ IT Office

⑫ PE Teachers' Office

⑬ General Services' Office

⑭ Accountants' Office

（3）活动室：

① Library

② Reading Room

③ Lecture Hall

④ Meeting Hall/Room

⑤ Teachers' Home

⑥ Psychological Consultation

⑦ Clinic

⑧ Studio

⑨ School History Room

（4）其他设施：

① Gatekeeper

② Security Office

③ Bulletin board

④ Reception Room

⑤ Printing Room

⑥ Resource Bank

⑦ Filing Room

⑧ Warehouse

⑨ Dining Hall

⑩ Dining Room(T)/(S)

⑪ Monitoring Center

⑫ Water Closet

⑬ Sports Storage Facility

⑭ Storeroom

6. Places off Campus

(1) laundry

(2) drudgery

(3) department store

(4) market

(5) zoo

(6) museum

(7) railway station

(8) shop

(9) book store

(10) gift shop

(11) library

(12) airport

(13) bus stop

(14) park

(15) fairground

(16) church

(17) post office

(18) police station

(19) fire station

(20) university

(21) botanic garden

(22) theater

(23) cinema

(24) art gallery

(25) stadium

(26) play ground

(27) bar

(28) office

(29) government

(30) shipside/dock/pier

(31) restaurant

(32) hotel

(33) shoemaker

(34) bakery

(35) gym

(36) subway station

(37) swimming pool

(38) tower

(39) café

(40) temple   (41) post office

✥ V. Basic Training

Exercise 2: Listen and Write down the Addresses You Hear [1]

1. _____

2. _____

3. _____

4. _____

Exercise 3: Listen to the Dialogues and Fill in the Form

Distinguish between a country and its nationality names, such as Germany/German, Italy/Italian. Listen to some people at an international conference and fill in the blanks. Some of them have been done for you. (Sequence: Name-Country-Nationality)

	Name	Country	Nationality		Name	Country	Nationality
1				6			Brazilian
2				7			Swedish
3	Francoise			8			Venezuelan
4	Carmen			9	Skouros		
5			Dutch	10	Ahmad		

Exercise 4: Listening Activity 1 [2]

In the UK the house number is given first and is followed by the name of the street. These two items are written on the same line. Next, the name of the city and county are written and are followed by the post code and the county if you are abroad.

Listen to the following dialogues and fill in the missing information in the spaces below.

1. My new address is 23 A _____ Road

   Ealing W5 London

   My telephone number is _____

---

1   https://www.tingclass.net/show-6697-114780-1.html
2   李亚宾 编著：《IELTS 考试技能训练教程——听力》，北京语言大学出版社，2007 年：第 5 页

2. My sister lives at _____ Avenue

   Nottingham

   Her telephone number is _____

3. My friend Alan lives in London. His address is _____ Road

   Ealing, London W5 5RF

   His telephone number is _____

4. My brother, Larry's address is _____

   His telephone number is _____

5. My parents live at _____

   Their telephone number is _____

6. My uncle George lives at _____

   His telephone number is _____

7. Mrs. Harper lives at _____

   Her telephone number is _____

8. Mr. Johnson lives at _____

   His telephone number is _____

Exercise 5: Listening Activity 2 [1]

Look at the diagram below and listen to the directions. As you listen, follow the directions and then write the appropriate number beside the name of each place.

The university library   _____

The supermarket   _____

The hotel   _____

The best bookshop   _____

The Lloyds Bank   _____

1 李亚宾 编著：《IELTS 考试技能训练教程——听力》，北京语言大学出版社，2007 年：第 44 页

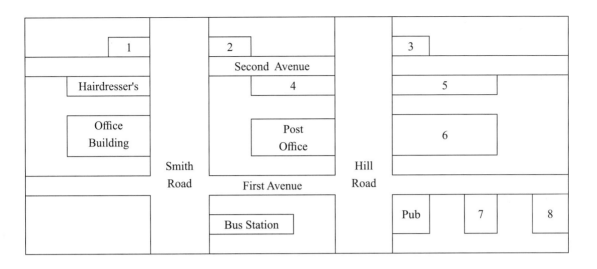

VI. Listening Skill 4—Maps and Plans

如何做地图题?

● 审题步骤:

1. 确认有无指南针

➤ 有指南针, speaker 往往会用 east, south, west 和 north 来表示方位, 同时, 要注意它们的形容词 eastern, southern, western 和 northern 以及复合方位词 southeast, southwest, northeast 和 northwest。

➤ 无指南针, speaker 往往会用头 top/up, bottom/down, left 和 right 来表示方位, 同时要注意 upper left/right corner, lower left/right corner 这样的表达。

➤ 中心地带往往用 center 来表示。

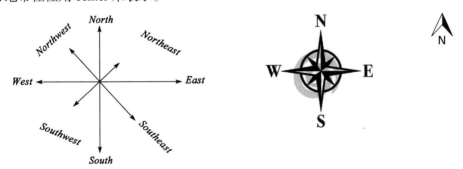

2. 确认从哪里出发

➤ 有时题目里会有一个人像或其它图形表示出发点，或者用一个圆圈或叉叉表示出发点，有时也会用英语 you are here，where we are 来表示 Speaker 所在的位置。

➤ 如果地图上没有上述图形，则需要仔细观察是否有车站、停车场或是大门、入口、接待处等标示。

➤ 如果上述两种情况都没有，则需要仔细听 Speaker 讲述所在方位。

3. 看清楚箭头走向

➤ 箭头走向标明 Speaker 即将讲述的行进方向，它会联系到后面题目的先后顺序。

➤ 如果转弯处有选项要特别注意。

4. 看清图上的标识

➤ 如果是户外的地图，尤其是自然环境下的地图，一般会在角落处标明各种图形所代表的含义，比如 tree, woods, river, pond, bridge 等；或者标明一些特别图形所代表的地点，比如铁轨、车道、步行道、车站、火车站等。

➤ 如果是室内的地图，可能也会有一些图示，比如 seating area, toilet 等。

➤ 另外，地图上的图形代表何种地点或建筑物，要注意特殊图形，比如一堆方块图形中的圆形、椭圆形。

➤ 要注意图形的布局，比如多个方块组成的品字形、一字形等。

5. 读题目中的已有单词

➤ 地图上已有的单词一定要事先默读一遍，加深印象。它们是参照物，起到地标作用，也是定位词。

6. 仔细阅读题干选项中的单词

➤ 题目中的单词要默读一遍，记住发音，以便于在听的时候能快速反应。

● **做题技巧：**

➤ 听清起点 / 出发点或所处位置，了解 Speaker 介绍的先后顺序，比如按箭头行走或者是顺时针方向介绍，按顺序行走，注意题号顺序。

➤ 掌握方位介词。

➤ 严格按照 Speaker 的指令，不要走得太快，尤其是过马路或者是过桥。

➤ 了解生活中的常见方位布局。

● 熟练掌握地道的方位表达

1. orientate yourselves around the site
   带你走一圈这个地方

2. in the reception area 在接待处

3. a corridor running left from here
   从这里左边有一条走廊

4. go along 沿着……走

5. face you at the end
   走到尽头，面对你的（那间房）

6. the entrance to the coffee room
   咖啡间的入口

7. the main road 主路

8. on one side 在一边

9. on the far side/end 远的那边 / 头（right）

10. next to（紧）靠着，（紧）挨着

11. go up the road to the turning area
    沿着马路向上走到转弯处

12. cross to the far side of the courtyard
    穿过庭院走到远的那一边

13. on your right/on the left/on people's right
    左手边 / 右手边

14. the last one on the right 右边最后一个

15. at the front of this building
    在这幢建筑物的前端

16. head to the left 朝左边走

17. the second room you come to
    你要走到第二个房间

18. go along the corridor past the courtyard,
    right to the end
    沿着走廊走，经过庭院，向右转走到底

19. you can see the river up in the north
    你可以看到北边上面那条河

20. near the entrance from the road
    在靠近马路的入口处附近

21. on the opposite side of the...
    在……的另一边（左右相对）

22. beyond the (line of) trees
    在（那排树的）外面

23. accessible by a footpath 步行道可以到

24. alongside the river 沿着河

25. in the southeast corner 在东南角

✄ VII. Note-taking Practice

Exercise 6: Listen and Copy [1]

1. I'm totally lost.

_____

2. Where are you headed?

_____

1　米山明日香、Catherine Dickson 著：《英式英语听力 4 周大特训》，众文图书公司，2016 年：第 100 页

3. Right, you should have kept going in the same direction.

_____

4. So I did take the wrong turning.

_____

5. You should go back the way you came.

_____

6. Then, when you're back on that street, turn right and keep going.

_____

7. Until I reach the hotel?

_____

8. That's right. You can't miss it.

_____

Exercise 7: Listen and Write the Key Information of Places in the Train Announcements [1]

1. _____
2. _____
3. _____
4. _____
5. _____
6. _____
7. _____
8. _____

---

1 闫先凤 编：《听力密码：听见英国》，中国水利水电出版社，2019 年：第 53 页

✨ VIII. Target Training

Exercise 8: IELTS Exercise—C14T2S2

Questions 11-15

Choose the correct letter, A, B or C.

Visit to Branley Castle

11. Before Queen Elizabeth I visited the castle in 1576,

A. repairs were carried out to the guest rooms.

B. a new building was constructed for her.

C. a fire damaged part of the main hall.

12. In 1982, the castle was sold to

A. the government.

B. the Fenys family.

C. an entertainment company.

13. In some of the rooms, visitors can

A. speak to experts on the history of the castle.

B. interact with actors dressed as famous characters.

C. see models of historical figures moving and talking.

14. In the castle park, visitors can

A. see an 800-year-old tree.

B. go to an art exhibition.

C. visit a small zoo.

15. At the end of the visit, the group will have

A. afternoon tea in the conservatory.

B. the chance to meet the castle's owners.

C. a photograph together on the Great Staircase.

Questions 16-20

Label the plan below. Write the correct letter A-I, next to Questions 16-20.

16. Starting point for walking the walls   _____

17. Bow and arrow display   _____

18. Hunting birds display   _____

19. Traditional dancing   _____

20. Shop   _____

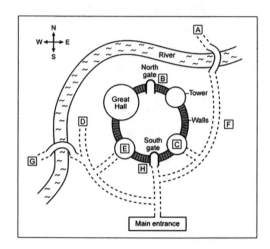

Exercise 9: IELTS Exercise—C15T2S2

Questions 11-14

Choose the correct letter, A, B or C.

Minster Park

11. The park was originally established

A. as an amenity provided by the city council.

B. as land belonging to a private house.

C. as a shared area set up by the local community.

12. Why is there a statue of Diane Gosforth in the park?

A. She was a resident who helped to lead a campaign.

B. She was a council member responsible for giving the public access.

C. She was a senior worker at the park for many years.

13. During the First World War, the park was mainly used for

A. exercises by troops.   B. growing vegetables.   C. public meetings.

14. When did the physical transformation of the park begin?

A. 2013   B. 2015   C. 2016

Questions 15-20

Label the map below. Write the correct letter, A-l, next to Questions 15-20.

15. statue of Diane Gosforth　　_____

16. wooden sculptures　　_____

17. playground　　_____

18. maze　　_____

19. tennis courts　　_____

20. fitness area　　_____

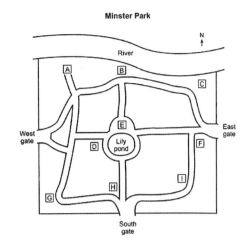

Minster Park

Exercise 10: IELTS Exercise—C15T4S2

Questions 11-16　Label the map below.

Write the correct letter. A-H, next to Questions 11-16.

Croft Valley Park

11. café　　_____

12. toilets　　_____

13. formal gardens　　_____

14. outdoor gym　　_____

15. skateboard ramp　　_____

16. wild lowers　　_____

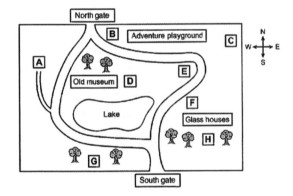

Questions 17 and 18

Choose TWO letters, A-E.

What does the speaker say about the adventure playground?

A. Children must be supervised.

B. It costs more in winter.

C. Some activities are only for younger children.

D. No payment is required.

E. It was recently expanded.

Questions 19 and 20

Choose TWO letters, A-E.

What does the speaker say about the glass houses?

A. They are closed at weekends.

B. Volunteers are needed to work there.

C. They were badly damaged by fire.

D. More money is needed to repair some of the glass.

E. Visitors can see palm trees from tropical regions.

IX. Listen and Understand the Culture

Exercise 11: Listen, Read and Speak

American English and British English [1]
美式英语和英式英语

George Bernard Shaw once said that England and America are two countries divided by a common language. Whereas this is true to a certain extent, and there is no doubt that many differences exist between these two forms of the same language, they are totally interchangeable. In other words, an American will understand 100% of what an English national says, and an English national will understand 100% of what an American says. People may have a little difficulty comprehending certain Regional slang words and phrases, etc., but the main gist of what is being said will be easily understood through context.

　　萧伯纳曾说，英国和美国是被一个共通语言分开的两个国家。虽然这话就某种程度上来说确实没错，而且这同一语言的两种形式之间确实存有许多差异，但这两种语言完全是可以互换的。换言之，一个美国人可以百分之百听懂一个英国人说的话，一个英国人也可以百分之百听懂一个美国人说的话。遇到某些地方性俚语和惯用语等用法时或许在理解上会有一点困难，不过通过上下文还是可以轻易了解话中的重点。

1　Christopher Belton 著：《英式英语的 32 堂听力课》，众文图书公司，2017 年 3 月：第 189 页

To compare American and British English to the Japanese language, it is not much different from the Kanto dialect and the Kansai dialect. The people from these areas speak with different accents and use: slightly different vocabularies in certain situations, but the basics of the language remain in place and communication is not a problem. However, it is interesting to imagine what would have become of British English and American English if we didn't live in the technological age. There is a very high possibility that both languages would have evolved in completely different ways if it were not for the mass media—radio, television and movies. From this point of view, we have to be thankful to the 20th century for keeping us moving down the same path hand in hand.

如果拿美式英语和英式英语同日语做比较的话，差别大概就像日语的关东方言和关西方言。来自这些地区的人说话时有各自的口音，在特定的情况下使用的字词也稍有不同，不过语言的基本架构是不变的，沟通也不成问题。然而，如果我们不是生活在科技时代，英式英语和美式英语会各自演变成什么样子，想想还蛮有趣的。如果没有收音机、电视机、电影等大众媒体，这两种语言形式极有可能会往完全不同的方向演变。从这个观点来看，还得感谢 20 世纪让它们得以携手走在同样的道路上呢。

The main differences between British English and American English are well known. The most obvious of these are the same spelling/different pronunciation words, such as "advertisement" and "schedule," and the different spelling/same pronunciation words，such as "colour," "cheque" and "defence." And, of course, we must not overlook the different words that are used for the same object, such as "petrol/gasoline", "lift/elevator" and "boot/trunk", etc. There are also a few grammatical differences that are worth mentioning. One is the tendency for British English to use the present perfect tense when describing an action that occurred in the recent past. For example, when refusing an invitation for lunch a British national would say "I have already eaten," whereas an American would say "I already ate." Another difference is the use of the words "have" and "got" to express possession. The British seem to be more at home with the word "got" and would say something like "Have you got a pencil I could borrow?" Americans, on the other hand, seem to prefer "have" and would ask the same question as "Do you have a pencil I could borrow?"

大家都很熟悉英式英语和美式英语之间主要的差异，其中最明显的就是拼写相同、发音不同的单词，例如 advertisement（广告）和 schedule（计划），另外还有拼写不同但发音相同的单词，例如 colour（颜色）、cheque（支票）、defence（防守）。当然，我们不能忽略那些长得不同，却用来表示同样物品的单词，例如 petrol 和 gasoline（汽油）、lift 和 elevator（电梯）、boot 和 trunk（汽车的后备厢）等。另外还有一些文法上的差异也值得一提，其一就是英式英语倾向用现在完成时来描述不久前发生的动作。举例来说，英国人拒绝他人的午餐邀约时会说 I have already eaten（我已经吃过了），美国人则会说 I already ate（我吃了）。另一个差异则是分别以 have 和 got 来表达拥有的状态。英国人似乎觉得用 got 比较自在，所以他们会说 Have you got a pencil I could borrow?（你有没有铅笔可以借我？）反之，美国人偏好用 have，所以同样的问题他们会说 Do you have a pencil I could borrow?

Whatever style of English you decide to study, it should be remembered that these differences account for only a tiny percentage of the entire language, and that either style can be used without problem in either country. English, after all, is English.

不管你决定学哪一种英语，应该要记住，这些差异只不过占整个语言的一个小小百分比，而且不论英式还是美式英语，在英美两国都行得通。英语毕竟就是英语。

What have you learnt from this passage?

1. New words

_____

_____

_____

2. Summary

_____

_____

_____

3. Your opinion

_____

_____

_____

Food and Drinks

Objectives:

● to know the British food and drinks

● to know the common expression of British food and drinks in daily life

● to know how to make some British food

● to practice the listening skill of understanding the intonations

● to know the British cuisine

I. Warm up

Exercise 1: Dictation of Words

1. _____	6. _____	11. _____	16. _____
2. _____	7. _____	12. _____	17. _____
3. _____	8. _____	13. _____	18. _____
4. _____	9. _____	14. _____	19. _____
5. _____	10. _____	15. _____	20. _____

🦋 II. Background Information [1]

British food has a good reputation, but English cooking has a bad one. It is difficult to explain the reason for this. Unfortunately, however, superb raw ingredients are often mined from the kitchen so that they come to the table without any of the natural flavor and goodness.

This bad reputation discourages a lot of people from eating in an English restaurant. If they do go to one, they are usually full of prejudice against the food. It is a pity, because there are excellent cooks in England, excellent restaurants, and excellent home-cooking. How, then, has the bad reputation been built up?

Perhaps one reason is that Britain's Industrial Revolution occurred very early, in the middle of the nineteenth century. As a result, the quality of food changed too. This was because Britain stopped being a largely agricultural country. The population of the towns increased enormously between 1840 and 1870, and people could no longer grow their own food, or buy it fresh from a farm. Huge quantities of food had to be taken to the towns, and a lot of it lost its freshness on the way.

This lack of freshness was disguised by "dressing up" the food. The rich middle classes ate long elaborate meals which were cooked for them by French chefs. French became, and has remained, the official language of the dining room. Out-of-season delicacies were served in spite of their expense, for there were a large number of extremely wealthy people who wanted to establish themselves socially. The "look" of the food was more important than its taste.

---

1   https://wangxiao.xisaiwang.com/tiku2/531287.html

In the 1930s, the supply of servant began to decrease. People still tried to produce complicated dishes, however, but they economized on the preparation time. The Second World War made things even worse by making raw ingredients extremely scarce. As a result, there were many women who never had the opportunity to choose a piece of meat from a well-stocked butcher's shop, but were content and grateful to accept anything that was offered to them.

Food rationing continued in Britain until the early 1950s. It was only after this had stopped, and butter, eggs and cream became more plentiful, and it was possible to travel abroad again and taste other ways of preparing food, that the English difference to eating became replaced by a new enthusiasm for it.

III. Testing Key Points[1]

雅思考试中，关于饮食的考点并不多，比较常见的是在住宿申请这个场景中，一方询问另一方的饮食喜好，比如要不要半膳宿、是不是素食主义者，或者有没有特别的饮食要求等。下面是在雅思真题里出现过的答案：

chocolate	meat	egg	refreshment
lentil curry	cheese	snack	chilled cola
coffee	seafood	free drink	

IV. Word Bank

Part 1 Food

● Fruits

1. pineapple 菠萝

2. watermelon 西瓜

3. banana 香蕉

4. orange 橙子

5. apple 苹果

6. lemon 柠檬

7. cherry 樱桃

8. peach 桃子

9. pear 梨

10. coconut 椰子

11. strawberry 草莓

12. raspberry 树莓

13. blueberry 蓝莓

14. blackberry 黑莓

---

1   https://www.oh100.com/kaoshi/danci/345167_4.html

15. grape 葡萄

16. sugar cane 甘蔗

17. mango 芒果

18. papaya 木瓜

19. apricot 杏子

20. nectarine 油桃

21. persimmon 柿子

22. pomegranate 石榴

23. durian 榴莲

24. kiwi fruit 猕猴桃

25. litchi 荔枝

● Vegetables

1. tomato 西红柿

2. potato 土豆

3. pumpkin 南瓜

4. sweet corn 甜玉米

5. lettuce 生菜、莴苣

6. Chinese cabbage 白菜

7. cabbage 甘蓝、卷心菜

8. radish 萝卜

9. carrot 胡萝卜

10. leek 韭菜

11. pea 豌豆

12. cucumber 黄瓜

13. onion 洋葱

14. celery 芹菜

15. mushroom 蘑菇

16. spinach 菠菜

17. eggplant 茄子

18. green pepper 青椒

19. lentil 扁豆

20. taro 芋头

21. yam 山药

● Meat

1. beef 牛肉

2. pork 猪肉

3. chicken 鸡肉

4. mutton 羊肉

5. lamb 羔羊肉

6. lean meat 瘦肉

7. speck 肥肉

8. pork joint 肘子

9. bacon 咸猪肉

10. steak 牛排

11. fillet 里脊肉

12. meat balls 肉丸子

● Sea food

1. lobster 龙虾

2. crayfish 小龙虾

3. crab 蟹

4. shrimp 小虾

5. prawn 对虾、大虾

6. squid 鱿鱼

7. oyster 牡蛎

8. jellyfish 海蜇

9. clam 蛤蜊

● Staple food

1. sandwich 三明治

2. rice 米饭

3. congee 粥

4. soup 汤

5. dumpling 饺子

6. noodle 面条

7. pizza 比萨饼

8. instant noodle 方便面

9. sausage 香肠

10. bread 面包

11. butter 黄油

12. cookies 饼干

13. pickle 咸菜（泡菜）

14. cake 饼（蛋糕）

15. hamburger 汉堡

16. ham 火腿

17. cheese 奶酪

18. flour 面粉

19. wheat 小麦

20. barley 大麦

21. oat 燕麦

22. dim sum 点心（中式）

23. egg tart 蛋挞

● Nuts

1. cashew nuts 腰果

2. peanut 花生

3. filbert hazel 榛子

4. chestnut 栗子

5. walnut 核桃

6. almond 杏仁

7. preserved fruit 果脯

8. raisin cordial 葡萄干

9. pistachio 开心果

Part 2 Drinks

1. beverage 酒水类

2. wine 红酒

3. brandy 白兰地

4. sherry 葡萄酒

5. beer 啤酒

6. vodka 伏特加

7. cocktail 鸡尾酒

8. soda
   汽水（软饮料）

9. juice 果汁

10. concentrated juice
    浓缩果汁

11. yoghurt 酸奶

12. soybean milk 豆浆

Part 3 Meals

1. breakfast 早餐   2. lunch 午餐   3. dinner 晚餐   4. brunch 早午餐

Part 4 Special Diet

1. special diet 特殊饮食

2. dietary requirement 饮食要求

3. vegetarian 素食

4. allergy 过敏

5. be allergic to 对……过敏

6. no meat 不吃肉

7. no red meat 不吃红肉

8. no nuts 不吃坚果

9. no seafood 不吃海鲜

10. dietary habit 饮食习惯

11. dietitian 饮食学家

Part 5 Seasonings

1. vinegar 醋

2. soy 酱油

3. salt 盐

4. sugar 糖

5. refined sugar 白糖

6. soy sauce 酱

7. salad 沙拉

8. hot(red)pepper 辣椒

9. (black)pepper 胡椒

10. seasoning 调料

11. sesame 芝麻

12. curry 咖喱粉

13. ketchup 番茄酱（汁）

14. spring onions 葱

15. ginger 姜

16. garlic 蒜　　　　18. aniseed 八角　　　　20. butter 黄油

17. oyster sauce 蚝油　　19. cinnamon 肉桂　　　21. vanilla extract 香草精

Part 6　Tastes

1. taste/flavour 品味　　4. sweet 甜的　　　7. spicy 辛辣的

2. salty 咸的　　　　　5. bitter 苦的　　　8. hot 热的；辣的

3. sugary 甜的　　　　6. sour 有酸味的　　9. spicy hot 辣热

Part 7　Ingredients

1. nutrition 营养　　　　6. sugar 糖　　　　11. carbohydrate 碳水化合物

2. nutrient 营养物质　　7. vitamin 维生素　　12. meal fibre 膳食纤维

3. ingredient 成分　　　8. fat 脂肪　　　　13. Sodium 钠

4. water 水　　　　　9. protein 蛋白质　　14. Calcium 钙

5. mineral 矿物质　　10. cholesterol 胆固醇　15. heat(kilocalorie) 热量（千卡）

Eat and Drink in London [1]

London has one of the most culturally diverse, exciting and fast-changing food scenes in the world. You are spoilt for choice; so much so that eating and drinking in London can be a bit overwhelming. We're here for you. Dive in and dine like a local with our regularly updated guides, hacks and insider tips.

● Cheap Eats

We love finding freebies and discounts for our fellow Cheapos but it's not all about price; we're also looking for great value for money. From a Michelin-starred lunch deals or bargain pre-theatre supper to the best dishes under a tenner , you might be spending money but we'll make sure you get the maximum bang for your buck.

● Types of Cuisine

Looking for something local or got your mind set on what you want to eat? We've got area guides and recommendations for everything from boozy brunches and fixed-price lunches to Friday night food cravings. So whether you're looking for a traditional British Sunday roast, good affordable sushi, or perhaps pasta in Islington or curry in Camden, you can relax and enjoy somewhere that's both local and fabulous.

1　https://londoncheapo.com/food-and-drink/

● Bars & Pubs

Thirsty Cheapos, we're not forgetting you —we'll not only point you to the best bars in town for cheap cocktails and the longest happy hours —we'll also share the cheapest places to drink without having to watch the clock. Maybe it's a late-night coffee shop you're after, or a traditional British pub beer garden? We've got you covered.

● Food Festivals & Events

Check out our Events section for more food and drink inspiration, from street food festivals and night markets to gin cruises and London Cocktail Week, in with all the other fun stuff that pops up in London all year round.

✿ V. Basic Training

Exercise 2 [1]

Listen to the recording and write down all the food and drinks you hear.

Food	Drinks

Exercise 3

Listen to the tape and choose the best answer. Listen again and write T if the statement is true and write F if the statement is false. [2]

1. At what age did John start his special diet?

A. 16　　　　　　　　　　B. 36　　　　　　　　　　C. 60

1　上田真理砂 & Iain Davey 著，葛窈君 译：《听见英国——英式英语实境听力练习》，众文图书公司，2021 年：第 274 页

2　上田真理砂 & Iain Davey 著，葛窈君 译：《听见英国——英式英语实境听力练习》，众文图书公司，2021 年：第 31 页

2. What freerange food does John eat?

A. Yogurt   B. Eggs   C. Chicken

3. Which of the following is NOT an example of a special food that John eats?

A. Tofu   B. Cheese   C. Beans

4. How long didn't John eat chicken or fish for?

A. 4 years   B. 5 years   C. 16 years

5. Why does John eat chicken and fish now?

A. His mother told him to.   B. It tastes good.   C. He isn't good at cooking.

6. John eats a lot of dairy products.

7. Freerange eggs are expensive and unhealthy.

8. Veggieburgers taste like vegetables.

9. John likes burgers made of nuts.

10. John lives with his mother.

Exercise 4

Listen to the tape and choose the best answer. Listen again and write T if the statement is true and write F if the statement is false. [1]

1. Which of the following is true?

A. Lager is darker than bitter.   B. Bitter is darker than lager.

C. Lager is stronger than bitter.   D. Bitter is stronger than lager.

2. What does Henrietta want to drink?

A. A pint of bitter.   B. Red wine.   C. Half a pint of shandy.   D. Half a pint of cider.

3. Why does Pete tell Henrietta to be careful?

A. Cider is strong.   B. Drinks are expensive.

C. Cider is more than half a litre.   D. She is driving.

1　上田真理砂 & Iain Davey 著，葛窈君 译：《听见英国——英式英语实境听力练习》，众文图书公司，2021 年：第 35 页

4. Who wants crisps?

A. Alan and Henrietta.　　　B. Henrietta.

C. Alan.　　　D. Neither of them.

5. What flavoured crisps did Pete first ask for?

A. Roast chicken.　　　B. Cheese and onion.

C. Prawn cocktail.　　　D. Roast beef.

6. Bitter is a traditional drink in England.

7. Cider is the same as apple juice.

8. Henrietta says she prefers shandy to cider.

9. Pete orders two packets of crisps.

10. Pete orders roast beef crisps.

Tips [1]

　　初次造访英国的人，或许会对怎么付钱这件事感到困惑。一般而言，在小酒馆向酒保点完饮料，就要直接付钱。

　　另外，结账时通常不会各付各的，而是由一个人付清全部的钱，等到下次再由其他人付账。因此，也常会遇到闲聊中被陌生人请喝一杯的情况。

Exercise 5: listen to the recording, understand the meanings of the idioms and do the matching.

1. there is no use crying over spilled milk

2. a good egg

3. walk on eggshells

4. you have to break some eggs to make an omelet

5. you are what you eat

6. meat and potatoes

7. one man's meat is another man's poison

A. you have to do what is necessary to move forward

B. A good diet is important for good health

C. the most important part of something or someone who likes simple things

D. you should not get angry when something bad happens and cannot be changed

E. a person who helps anyone in need.

F. have to be careful about what we said or did

G. one person might like something very much while another person might hate the same thing

1　米山明日香、Catherine Dickson 著：《英式英语听力 4 周大特训》，众文图书公司，2016 年：第 100 页

8. the salt of the earth	H. a good and honest person
9. pour salt on a wound	I. very tall
10. take it with a grain of salt	J. make someone feel worse about something that was already a painful experience
11. brings home the bacon	
12. cut the mustard	K. not believe everything he told us.
13. tall drink of water	L. made a big mistake and felt foolish
14. packed like sardines	M. do not like
15. out to lunch	N. something to think about
16. there is no such thing as a free lunch	O. do what is expected of him at work
	P. so crowded
17. wake up and smell the coffee	Q. out of touch and not always know what is going on in our office
	R. something may appear to be free of charge, but there may be a hidden cost
18. egg on my face	
19. not my cup of tea	S. need to pay more attention and fix the problem
20. food for thought	T. make enough money to support family

❦ VI. Listening Skill 5—Understanding the Intonation[1]

● 了解重读、停顿和拖音背后的含义。

● 抓住语调变换，判断肯定或否定的态度。

　　考生在备考雅思听力的过程中，在语音语调方面所要解决的问题主要有以下几个方面：

　　1. 词义与语音之间的联系。如果考生在听到单词发音时无法迅速将其转化为相应的意思，则会造成听力考试中很大的障碍，读不对必定听不懂。因此，考生在准备雅思听力单词的时候，必须在语音与词义之间建立联系，不能单纯地机械记忆单词拼写，而是要一边听单词书配备的录音一边背。"语言是音、义结合的词汇和语法体系"；"语音是语言的物质外壳，语义是语言的意义内容"。

　　2. 掌握连读、失去爆破、弱音，区分近音的干扰。单词的读音是由元音和辅音有规则地结合在一起形成的。每一个元音或辅音都会被邻近的发音影响，而每一个元音又会受到其所在的音节结构的影响。考生在考试中觉得"听不清"有时正是因为这些发音现象。为了解决这个问题，考生首先应该了解各个音标的正确发音，其次对连读、失去爆破、语音同化、弱化等发音现象进行辨别、跟读，以增强敏感性。此外，考生还可以对听力材料进行听写练习，听不出来的地方再对照原文分析其特殊的发音现象。

1　http://www.zhld.com/content/2010-10/22/content_59801.htm

3. 当听力录音中出现重读时，说话人往往强调这一点，其中的关键信息也是听力题目的提问点。因此，考生在听录音时必须掌握语句中的重音。雅思听力考试是以考查考生的交际性为特色的。众所周知，在日常谈话中，任何重读往往都是说话人想要强调的。然而，大多数考生为了理解每个单词而忽略了重读词，导致漏听或错误理解材料的意思，得不偿失。

4. 语调指的是声音的高低起伏，通常以句子为单位。加上语调的句子能清楚表达说话者的意思。简单来说，语调下降代表句子的完结、确定，语调上扬则带有询问、继续之义。因此，语调用错的话，听的人会误解句子的意思。换句话说，对话时有必要从语调来了解说话者的意思。例如，在飞机上，空服人员如果说"Fish (/) or meat (\)?"，表示要请乘客"从鱼或肉当中选择一样主餐"，如果语调是"Fish (/) or meat (/)?"，则暗示可能有鱼或肉以外的选择。

也就是说，多个选项并列时，最后的选项如果是语调下降，表示要对方从现有的选项中挑出一个；如果语调上扬，则代表还有其他的选项。具体来说，假设有 A 到 E 五个选项，而语调为"A (/)，B (/)，C (/)，D (/) and/or E (\)?"，通常就是五选一的模式。

请记住这个规则，进行语调的练习吧。

Practice

1. Tom or Bob(\)?

2. Tom or Bob(/)?

3. Apple, orange or carrot(\)?

4. Apple, orange or carrot(/)?

5. Coffee, tea, espresso or cappuccino(\)?

6. Coffee, tea, espresso or cappuccino(/)?

7. We will visit Big Ben, the Houses of Parliament, London Bridge and London Eye(\).

8. We will visit Big Ben, the Houses of Parliament, London Bridge and London Eye(/).

9. I would like tomato, ham, egg and salami(\).

10. I would like tomato, ham, egg and salami(/).

11. Cheddar, mozzarella, blue cheese or cream cheese(\)?

12. Cheddar, mozzarella, blue cheese or cream cheese(/)?

13. Would you prefer blue, pink, yellow, green or brown(\)?

14. Would you prefer blue, pink, yellow, green or brown(/)?

✺ VII. Notetaking Practice

Exercise 6: Listen and Copy [1]

1. I'd like a tuna sandwich, please.

_____

2. Eat in or take away?

_____

3. What toppings would you like?

_____

4. We've got tomatoes, lettuce, cucumber...

_____

5. I'll have a bit of everything, thanks.

_____

6. Would you like anything to drink with that?

_____

7. Small, medium or large?

_____

8. That looks delicious. Thanks.

_____

Exercise 7: Listen and Write [2]

1. _____
2. _____
3. _____
4. _____
5. _____
6. _____
7. _____
8. _____

---

1 米山明日香、Catherine Dickson 著：《英式英语听力 4 周大特训》，众文图书公司，2016 年：第 43 页
2 闫先凤 编：《听力密码：听见英国》，中国水利水电出版社，2019 年：第 66 页

✍️ VIII. Target Training

Exercise 8: Organic Chocolate [1]

Listen to the recording and fill the blanks to complete the sentences with NO MORE THAN THREE WORDS AND/OR A NUMBER.

Part 1

1. Chocolate is made from cocoa beans and farmers spend long time looking after and _____ the crops.

2. Many farmers use _____ to help their crops grow and to kill the insect pests that attack the plants, or turn to traditional methods.

3. The farmers have to spend a lot more time looking after their crops. They have to protect them from _____ and insect pests.

Part 2

4. Experts say that the ancient Aztec communities in _____ first used cocoa beans for payment or to make a special _____.

5. In ancient times chocolate was linked to power, _____ and love. People believed that chocolate helped them think more _____. Some people even believed that chocolate had special _____ powers.

6. The sailors in 16th century decided to bring them back to _____. And then people drink it with _____.

7. Sweet chocolate was thought to cure _____ disease. Others said that it made the _____ look better. And it would stop people from getting _____!

Part 3

8. The reason why chocolate makes people happy is that there are special _____ in chocolate, which react with a person's _____.

9. Organic farming ensures that the _____ are kept and developed and it is beneficial for the growth of the cocoa beans.

---

1 https://www.tingclass.net/show-8483-240150-1.html?gfh

10. Organic farming helps develop Venezuela's _____ industry. It increases the countries' _____ wealth. The government has given around _____ to encourage organic farming.

Exercise 9: World Food Day [1]

Listen to the recording and fill the note below with NO MORE THAN THREE WORDS AND/OR A NUMBER.

Telefood Project

People in hunger

- More than 1. _____ people in the world do have enough to eat.
- Hunger and 2. _____ claim twenty 25,000 lives every day.

Media report

- There are reports about new 3. _____ and papers to end world hunger.
- Food aid comes and disappears in needy countries. Problems remain.
- Political conflict and 4. _____ caused the food problem in local villages and young girls raise 5. _____ for food.

Telefood project

- Telefood is part of the FAO—the UN's Food and Agriculture Organization which launched Telefood in 6. _____.
- With their help, poor villages sell 7. _____ and chickens to the whole community at reasonable prices.
- Telefood also provided the necessary materials to grow 8. _____ and vegetables because many local farmers lack 9. _____ to grow crops in their fields.
- 10. _____ are the main providers of food for their families.

---

1   https://www.tingclass.net/show-8482-239945-1.html?gfh

Exercise 10

Listen to the recording and complete the sentences below with NO MORE THAN TWO WORDS. [1]

Pizza: A Cultural Food

1. Pizza is a food made by putting meat and vegetables, called _____.

2. In Brazil, _____ are popular on pizza.

3. In Japan, food from the _____, like eel and squid are popular.

4. In Costa Rica, people enjoy the _____ fruit on top of their pizzas.

5. In Italy, the bread, or _____, of the pizza is the most important part.

6. A popular pizza in the Netherlands is called the "_____." It has two times the cheese, two times the onions, and two times the beef.

7. As you can see, there are many different ways to eat pizza. A food that is popular in one culture will not always be popular in another culture. But pizza seems to cross all these _____.

8. Experts do agree that the design, or _____, for modern pizza was probably put together using different ideas from different cultures.

9. Middle Eastern cultures had something similar to pizza. People there would add _____ and good tasting spices to the bread. Then they cooked this flat, spiced bread in hot ovens. It was a small food that people ate between meals. Or they added it to a meal.

10. Another version of this flat round bread was also popular in _____. The local people called it "plankuntos." They put vegetables and meat on top of the flat bread.

---

1   https://www.tingclass.net/show-8483-250141-1.html

Exercise 11

Listen to the recording and complete the notes below with NO MORE THAN TWO WORDS. [1]

The World's Favourite Food: Bread

- Bread is one of the world's oldest foods, starting thousands of years ago, a long time before 1. _____ facts.

- Wheat is the main part, or 2. _____, in most bread.

- Two groups in ancient 3. _____ and Mesopotamia (part of modern Iraq) were first to eat such food. When they cooked it, the bread was sometimes softer and lighter and this was caused by yeast which created 4. _____.

- Today, many people visit the 5. _____ in London where they can see bread in a king's funeral building.

- In the ancient Roman Empire, bread-making had become a real skill. The bakers enjoyed special treatment:

- they were not 6. _____

- they could not mix with some people — 7. _____ and fighters

- being a baker was a job for life

- Over the years, the main ingredients of bread have not changed much. However, different cultures have created their own versions.

- Pitta: a small round flat bread eaten in Middle Eastern countries.

- Baguette: a long thin stick of white bread, very popular with 8. _____ people.

- Roggenbrot: a popular black bread in 9. _____.

- Injera: a bread made from teff with water and cooked in oil.

- Years ago, bread was also a sign of someone's 10. _____. It takes a number of processes to make the wheat as white as possible.

1 https://www.tingclass.net/show-8483-251571-1.html

🎵 IX. Listen and Understand the Culture

Exercise 12: Listen, Read and Speak

British Cuisine [1]
英国菜

British cuisine is the specific set of cooking traditions and practices associated with the United Kingdom. British cuisine has been described as "unfussy dishes made with quality local ingredients, matched with simple sauces to accentuate flavor, rather than disguise it." However, British cuisine has absorbed the cultural influence of those who have settled in Britain, producing many hybrid dishes, such as the AngloIndian chicken tikka masala.

英国的美食是英国传统烹调和实践的具体结合。英国菜被描述为："由当地的优质食材制成的普通菜，配以简单的酱汁突出风味，而不是掩盖其口味。"然而，英国菜系已经受到移民带来的外来文化的影响，推出了许多混合型菜肴，如印度咖喱鸡块。

Celtic agriculture and animal breeding produced a wide variety of foodstuffs for indigenous Celts and Britons. AngloSaxon England developed meat and savory herb stewing techniques before the practice became common in Europe. The Norman conquest introduced exotic spices into England in the Middle Ages. The British facilitated a knowledge of India's elaborate food tradition of "strong, penetrating spices and herbs". Food rationing policies, put in place by the British government during wartime periods of the 20th century, are said to have been the stimulus for British cuisine's poor international reputation.

1　闫先凤 编：《听力密码：听见英国》，中国水利水电出版社，2019 年：第 176 页

凯尔特人的农业与畜牧业推出了各种各样的凯尔特和英国土著食品。盎格鲁—撒克逊英格兰推出的香草炖肉技术在欧洲非常普遍。中世纪时，诺尔曼征服将异国香料引入英格兰。英国采用了印度人用香料和草药精心制作美食的传统，促进了知识的传承。据说在 20 世纪的战争时期，英国政府的食品配给政策刺激到了英国菜糟糕的国际声誉。

British cuisine has traditionally been limited in its international recognition to the full breakfast, fish and chips, and the Christmas dinner. Other British dishes include the Sunday roast, steak and kidney pie, shepherd's pie, and bangers and mash. British cuisine has many regional varieties within the broader categories of English, Scottish and Welsh cuisine. Each have developed their own regional or local dishes, many of which are geographically indicated foods such as Cornish pasties, the Yorkshire pudding, Cumberland sausage and Welsh cakes.

闻名于世的传统英国菜包括全套早餐、炸鱼和薯条，以及圣诞晚宴。其他菜包括星期日烤牛肉、牛腰子派、肉馅土豆饼、香肠和土豆泥。英国菜的类别由于英格兰、苏格兰和威尔士许多地方美食的加入已经更为丰富。每个地区都开发了自己的地方菜，其中许多是地方性食品，例如康瓦尔郡菜肉烘饼、约克郡布丁、坎伯兰香肠和威尔士蛋糕。

Modern British (or New British) cuisine is a style of British cooking which fully emerged in the late 1970s, and has become increasingly popular. It uses highquality local ingredients, preparing them in ways which combine traditional British recipes with modern innovations. Much of Modern British cooking also draws heavily on influences from Mediterranean cuisines, and more recently, Middle Eastern, South Asian, East Asian and Southeast Asian cuisines. The traditional influence of northern and central European cuisines is significant but fading.

现代英国（或新英伦）菜是英国烹饪在 20 世纪 70 年代后期风格的充分体现，并越来越受到欢迎。它采用高品质的食材，把英国传统配方与现代创新方式相结合。许多现代英国烹饪在很大程度上受到了地中海地区美食的影响，最近也受到了中东、南亚、东亚和东南亚美食的影响。传统的北欧和中欧美食的影响虽然意义深远但却日趋衰落。

What have you learnt from this passage?

1. New words

_____

_____

_____

2. Summary

_____

_____

_____

3. Your opinion

_____

_____

_____

Game Time:

Watch a video and learn about the process of making a sandwich.

https://www.tingclass.net/show98813741931.html

Transportation

Objectives:

● to know the different modes of transportation

● to know the special situations related in real life, such as taking transportations and renting a car, and local transportation around the world

● to learn about the future of cars

● to learn about the listening skill—catching the nouns

● to know the driving left rule in UK

 I. Warm up

Exercise 1: Dictation of Words

1. _____   6. _____   11. _____   16. _____

2. _____   7. _____   12. _____   17. _____

3. _____   8. _____   13. _____   18. _____

4. _____   9. _____   14. _____   19. _____

5. _____   10. _____   15. _____   20. _____

✒ II. Background Information—Underground in London[1]

For the visitor to London the Underground or Tube will probably be the transport of choice to get around town. The Underground is normally the fastest way to get around town, often much faster than any taxi.

There is invariably an underground station nearby where you want to go and also your hotel (there are currently 12 Underground lines) and finding your way around the system is very easy.

- ## Key points about the London Underground

During the Coronavirus pandemic you MUST wear a face covering at all times when using public transport and follow all the rules to keep yourself and others as safe as possible.

The authorities penalise you heavily for buying single journey tickets. In the centre you can pay more than double the price than if you used an Oyster Card for example.

A single journey on the London Underground can involve 1 or 2 changes of train. Your journey starts when you go through the ticket barrier of the station entrance you depart from and finishes when you pass through the ticket barrier at the exit of your destination. You cannot break a journey on a single fare, once you go through an exit barrier of a station that is journey completed.

The buses, Underground, DLR and London suburban trains are managed by a central government body called Transport for London (TfL) chaired by the Mayor of London. The transport passes that nearly everyone uses, Oyster and Travelcard, allow you to travel seamlessly across all modes of transport, bus, Underground, train and DLR using the same ticket/pass.

---

1   https://www.britannica.com/topic/London-Underground

Children under 11 travel free on the London Underground and DLR (Docklands Light Railway) at all times. Child fares are available for those under 16 and it is possible to get discounted fares if you are under 18 or studying in London with an ID card.

There are no seniors fares for visitors. If you reside in London and are over 60 you can get a pass that makes free bus and Underground travel available. If you have an English National Concessionary bus pass you cannot use it on the London Underground (but you can use it on London's red buses).

The London Underground is closed from around midnight until around 5 am, getting started a little later on Sundays. However on Friday and Saturday nights, much of the Underground runs through the night. In Central London there is a very good night bus network when the Underground is closed.

You will rarely have to wait more than 5 minutes for an Underground train at any time of the day.

- London Underground map

The London Underground map is a classic design that when first launched was immediately taken up worldwide for similar systems. The clarity, simplicity and ease of use compromises strict geographical accuracy. The Circle line doesn't really go around in a squashed circle and it is not apparent for instance that Bayswater Underground is only 100 yards from Queensway.

In 2016 the Night Tube was introduced. On Friday and Saturday nights only Underground trains run through the night. For lines that operate a night service see the Night Tube map linked below or on the right-menu.

- London Underground fares

➢ **Fare zones**

The London public transport system is divided up into zones that radiate from the centre. Nearly all the hotels and the main sights are in Zone 1. Heathrow Airport is in Zone 6 and the furthest zone out is Zone 9.

The majority of visitors will only travel in the two most central zones 1 and 2. The Underground Map (link above) has the stations and their zones marked.

Some stations, such as Turnham Green, are in two zones. You use whichever zone for these stations is most beneficial in working out your fare.

> **Underground fares**

You can see from the table below there is big financial incentive not to purchase individual tickets and use an Oyster card or Contactless payment card.

The other main way of paying is purchasing a Travelcard, which is a pass giving you unlimited travel for a set time period. The cost goes up with the coverage of zones required. The more zones you require the more expensive the Travelcard.

● Oyster cards, Contactless payment cards & Travelcards

As you can see from the above fare structure the authorities do not want you to buy single tickets, they want you to purchase one of the three payment options, Oyster cards, Contactless payment cards or Travelcards.

London Underground Fares 2021

Zones Travelled	Single Journey Ticket		Oyster / Contactless Payment Card~	
	Adult	Child†	Peak*	Off Peak
Zone 1	£5.50	£2.70	£2.40	£2.40
Zone 1 & 2	£5.50	£2.70	£3.00	£3.00
Zone 1 to 3	£5.50	£2.70	£3.40	£2.80
Zone 1 to 4	£6.00	£3.00	£4.00	£2.90
Zone 1 to 5	£6.00	£3.00	£4.80	£3.20
Zone 1 to 6	£6.00	£3.00	£5.30	£3.30
Zone 2 to 6	£6.00	£3.00	£5.30	£3.30

No return fares.

† Children travel free if under 11 year old or are between 11 and 15 years with an Oyster 11-15 Photocard

~ Children's fares (11-15 yrs old) on Oyster for any trip within zones 1 to 6 are £0.75 off peak, £0.85 peak

* Peak fares apply Monday to Friday between 6.30am and 9.30am and 4pm to 7pm, except public holidays

The Oyster card is a permanent reusable electronic ticket which is topped up from time to time by its owner. Londoners also have their season tickets loaded onto Oyster cards as well and there are passes for one weekly and monthly durations. All can be loaded onto the one electronic Oyster card.

Contactless cards are standard credit or debit cards that support the contactless payment technology, the total cost of all the journeys that you make in one day is calculated at the end of the day and a single charge is made to your Contactless payment card account.

Unlike the Oyster card the contactless facility has a 7-day cap as well as the Oyster daily cap used by Oyster.

You can use Oyster cards on all of London's public transport, not just the Underground, but buses, overground, DLR, suburban rail services and some river services.

Travelcards are another alternatives. Travelcards are valid on the same modes of transport but are unlimited travel passes for a fixed flat fee. Travelcards are available for 1 and 7 days, 1 month and 1 year durations.

You can purchase and subsequently top up Oyster cards and Travelcards from Underground stations and a wide variety of other outlets throughout London including neighbourhood stores, but not Contactless payment cards.

Tube map

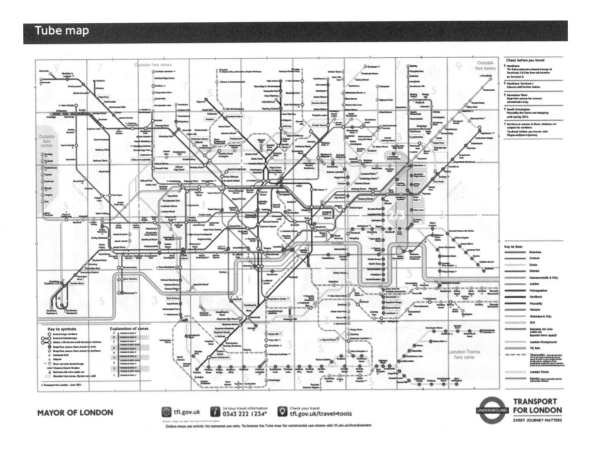

MAYOR OF LONDON

TRANSPORT FOR LONDON
EVERY JOURNEY MATTERS

III. Testing Key Points

交通运输的考点在雅思考试中经常出现在旅游场景中，其中涉及交通出行的方式，比如乘坐大巴、自驾游等，还会考到乘坐的人数、出行的时间和班次、停车的地点等。除此以外，也有关于交通运输情况的调查，比如路线、车次数量、车况、车费等。

在日常生活中，交通运输的话题还涉及一些服务，比如租车、修车、车辆买卖、考驾照或者是违反交通规则被罚等事宜。

IV. Word Bank

Bus

1. double decker bus　双层公共汽车

2. coach　大客车

3. taxi, cab　出租车

4. trolley bus　无轨电车

5. tram　电车，有轨电车

6. underground, tube, subway　地铁

7. stop　停车站

8. taxi rank, taxi stand　计程汽车车站

9. taxi driver, cab driver 出租车司机

10. conductor 售票员

11. inspector 检查员，稽查员

12. ride 乘车

13. minimum fare (of a taxi) 最低车费

Railway

1. track 轨道

2. railway system, railway net-work 铁路系统

3. express train 特别快车

4. fast/slow train 快 / 慢车

5. excursion train 游览列车

6. commuter train, suburban train 市郊火车

7. carriage 车厢

8. dining car, restaurant car, luncheon car 餐车

9. berth, bunk 铺位

10. luggage van, baggage car 行李车

11. station hall 车站大厅

12. booking office, ticket office 售票处

13. platform 月台，站台

14. left-luggage office 行李暂存处

15. terminal, terminus 终点站

16. rack, baggage rack 行李架

17. left-luggage office 行李房（美式：checkroom）

18. timetable 时刻表

19. change, transfer 换乘

20. ticket inspector 验票员

21. to change trains at... 在（某地）换车

22. the train is due at... 在（某时）到达

23. to break the journey 中途下车

Boat, Ship

1. (passenger) liner 邮轮，客轮

2. sailing boat, sailing ship 帆船

3. yacht 游艇

4. cabin 船舱，客舱

5. hovercraft 气垫船

6. life buoy 救生圈

7. lifeboat 救生艇

8. life jacket 救生衣

9. first-class cabin 头等舱

10. gang-plank 跳板

11. crossing 横渡

12. cruise 游弋

13. to land 抵岸

14. on board a ship, aboard 在船上

15. to stop over at... 中途在……停留

Plane, Aircraft, Airplane

1. jet 喷气机

2. airline 航空公司

3. customs formalities 报关单

4. boarding pass 登机牌

5. air terminal 航空集散站，停机场

6. air hostess, stewardess/steward 空中小姐，女乘务员 / 乘务员

7. aircraft crew, air crew 机组，机务人员

8. pilot 驾驶员，机长

9. takeoff 起飞

10. landing 着陆

11. to board a plane, get into a plane 上飞机

12. to get off a plane, alight from a plane 下飞机

13. non-stop flight to 飞往，直飞

14. in transit 运送中的

● 雅思听力中出现过的其他交通工具

minibus 小型公共汽车　　　shuttle bus 豪华轿车　　　ferry 渡船　　　cab 出租车

coach 长途汽车　　　　　　horse 马　　　　　　　donkey 驴　　　camel 骆驼

V. Basic Training

Exercise 2: Bus Travel [1]

Listen to the recording and judge whether the statement is true or false.

1. The bus to Reno, Nevada, leaves at 9:15 a.m.

2. The bus to Boise, Idaho, arrives at 9:35 p.m.

3. The bus fare to Reno, Washington, is one hundred twelve dollars.

4. The bus bound for Fresno, California, leaves at 11 O'clock sharp.

5. The bus heading to Reno is scheduled to arrive at half past 4:00.

6. The bus fare to Boston is eighty-five dollars.

7. The bus to Seattle is scheduled to arrive at ten after five.

8. The bus to Seattle leaves 20 minutes earlier than the bus to Boise.

9. The bus fare to Fresno is just under a hundred dollars.

10. The bus trip to Reno takes over seven hours.

Exercise 3: Taking A Bus [2]

Listen to the tape and answer the questions.

1. Which bus did Megumi need to take to get to Hyde Park?

1　https://www.baidu.com/link?url=Jc3f3-9UX7adDUI3W5XBk_PVDhBF_GaZyX9qgUXKZBZAtPCiMQJIew-Lmv-As-0EK91_t0Q7GeJww0Y30V2B-K&wd=&eqid=e6e776fd000208a00000000363eb1e4b

2　米山明日香、Catherine Dickson 著：《英式英语听力 4 周大特训》，众文图书公司，2016 年：第 49 页

2. What is a Routemaster?

_____

3. Can she use her Oyster card on the bus?

_____

4. Which train station did she pass?

_____

5. When she wanted to get off the bus, what did she do?

_____

Tips:

搭乘巴士（叭叭走）[1]

一提到伦敦，几乎就会联想到 double-decker（双层巴士）。大红色的双层巴士可说是伦敦交通工具的代名词，造访伦敦时绝对会想搭乘体验看看。近年来除了红色巴士，还随处可见车体包覆广告、色彩缤纷的双层巴士。

不过，一般观光客常因为不熟悉搭乘方式而对这些双层巴士敬而远之。其实，游客可事先至 Transport for London 网站查询路线图，只要输入所在地与目的地，就可以轻松获得搭乘信息。巴士站牌都有清楚标示巴士号码，只要确定了号码和目的地就可以上车了。

最近巴士也跟上现代化的脚步，让观光客在搭乘上更方便了。除了车上广播变成自动播放系统，车上还设置了显示目的地的电子屏幕，若听不懂广播还可以看电子屏幕上显示的信息，不用担心下错站。双层巴士在最早的 Routemaster 年代，播报站名的是售票员（conductor）而非司机，但因为这些人多半有很重的伦敦口音（Cockney），常常让外国观光客难以理解。另外，一般搭乘巴士是上车投币；使用牡蛎卡的话，金额直接从卡片里扣除，用起来也十分方便。

Exercise 4: Traffic Problem [2]

Listen to the recording and complete the note below with ONLY ONE WORD OR A NUMBER.

Busy London

- London is a center of government and 1. _____.
- More than 2. _____ people live in the greater London area.

---

1 米山明日香、Catherine Dickson 著：《英式英语听力 4 周大特训》，众文图书公司，2016 年：第 55 页

2 https://www.tingclass.net/show-8483-249371-1.html

- London still shows signs of this long 3. _____.
- Many streets are 4. _____, and they were not designed for cars.

A new idea—A congestion charge

- A congestion charge is a 5. _____ to take a vehicle into Central London.
- 6. _____ record the license plate numbers—the registration numbers of the cars to catch and
7. _____ people who have not paid the charge.
- The goal of a congestion charge is to stop some people from using their cars.

Views on the effects of the congestion charge

- The city authorities:
- The charge has helped. There are fewer cars on the road in Central London.
- Traffic travelled faster. After the charge, the average speed increased to 8. _____.
- 9. _____ quality improved.

- Not everyone agrees
- Some people who live in the city 10. _____ about the charge.
- Some people argue that it has not really improved the traffic.

Exercise 5

Listen to the recording and choose the best answer.

The History of Bicycle

'Pushbikes' —The first bicycle
- The first working bicycle was in the early 1800's.
- The first bicycle had 1. _____.
- But it did not have 2. _____.

'Boneshaker' —in the 1850's and 60's

● French inventors changed the design of the bicycle.

- The front wheel was larger

- The bicycle had a heavy 3. _____ frame

- The wheels were made of 4. _____ and iron

'The ordinary' —over the next ten years

● Inventors changed the design of the bicycle even more.

- They increased its 5. _____

- They also added 6. _____ tires on the wheels

- But these kinds of bicycles were difficult to ride.

The first modern bicycle—in 1885

● J.K. Starley invented the first modern bicycle.

- Front and back wheels were similar sized

- A thin metal 7. _____ was added to change directions.

- A better 8. _____ was also added

● More improvements

- Better 9. _____ was used for the wheels.

- Good 10. _____ was used to stop the bicycle.

❧ VI. Listening Skill 6—Catching the Nouns

在备考前，考生不妨做个听力模拟练习，了解一下自己的听力水平，不同的听力水平考生应该设定不同的听力练习计划和方法。如果本身听力基础不错，考生可以直接进入听力专项练习，而不需要额外补充听力词汇。但本身英语基础比较薄弱的考生，备考计划应更加详细全面。

刚开始做雅思真题时，考生可以适当做些听写练习。雅思真题就是很好的听写材料。具体如下：

1. 第一遍听写：记录整个听力内容的概要及关键信息点，并标记出自己的听力盲点。

2. 第二遍听写：分句听写。这个过程考生可反复 3 ~ 4 遍进行，直到整个句子听写完整。

3. 第三遍听写：核对听写内容。

在听力中，名词往往是最关键的信息，也往往是答案。所以，考生需要强化抓音听写名词的能力。名词主要出现的位置主要是句首（作主语）和句中（作宾语、表语、补语等），通常在冠词（a, an, the）、代词（my, this, some, another 等）、介词（of, in, with 等）、及物动词（see, eat, expect 等）和数词（one, first, half 等）后面，写答案的时候需要注意可数名词的单复数。

Practice

请同学们两两分组，老师分发两份不同的朗读段落，一个同学朗读一段文字，另一个同学把里面的**名词**全部记录下来，然后检查核对。接下来，轮换进行。

_____
_____
_____
_____
_____
_____
_____

✐ VII. Note-taking Practice

Exercise 6: Listen and Copy [1]

1. So we use our oyster cards before we get on the train, right?

_____

2. There are a lot of lines here: yellow, red, green, brown...

_____

3. There's a colour chart at the bottom... look.

_____

4. The trains come every few minutes, so we won't have to wait long.

_____

1　米山明日香、Catherine Dickson 著：《英式英语听力 4 周大特训》，众文图书公司，2016 年：第 23 页

5. Please mind the gap between the train and the platform.

_____

6. How long will it take to get into central London?

_____

7. Please change here for the District Line.

_____

8. Let passengers off the train first, please.

_____

Exercise 7: Listen and Write [1]

1. _____
2. _____
3. _____
4. _____
5. _____
6. _____
7. _____
8. _____

❧ VIII. Target Training

Exercise 8

The Advantages of Using Bicycles

Main form of transport

- Bicycles helped people get from place to place easier.

- Riding a bicycle is faster than walking.
- Scientists and inventors made better 1. _____, like Henry Ford and the Wright Brothers

---

1 闫先凤 编：《听力密码：听见英国》，中国水利水电出版社，2019 年：第 81 页

Effects on societies

- The bicycle changed life for 2. _____ in many ways.
- They wore 3. _____ like men usually wear.
- Bicycles made them feel more 4. _____ and expected freedom and respect.

Effects on the lives of people in cities

- They helped reduce 5. _____ in cities.
- Bicycles also made it easier for people to meet and 6. _____.

Many things have changed

Bicycles continue to be a popular form of transportation in many parts of the world because:

- Inventors have made great improvements to the bicycle.
- Today's bicycles are easy to ride and much more 7. _____.
- And they can go very fast.

Many good reasons to ride a bicycle

- Bicycles do not damage the 8. _____.
- Riding bicycles is good for health.
- Bicycles cost less money to ride and 9. _____.

Many cities in China and the 10. _____ contain more bicycles than cars.

Exercise 9: Local Transport Around the World [1]

Listen to the recording and complete the note below with ONLY ONE WORD OR A NUMBER.

_____

1   https://www.tingclass.net/show-8491-240725-1.html?gfh

Part 1

Local Transport Around the World (1)

Taxis

- 1. _____ taxis in New York

- Black taxis in 2. _____

Jeepney in the Philippines

- A very special form of transport, made from jeeps, which were US 3. _____ vehicles to drive in difficult conditions, like damaged roads, 4. _____ roads, and forest roads

- Longer and removed unwanted parts

- Add a 5. _____ top to protect the passengers from the sun and rain

- Price was very 6. _____

- Wait for a long time if it is not full unless a passenger pays for the 7. _____ seats

- Painted with 8. _____ colours

- Add small objects to the front, such as lights, and 9. _____, and pictures and poems inside

- Government has made the drives set 10. _____ prices

Part 2

Local Transport Around the World (2)

Tuk-tuks in Thailand

- 11. _____ vehicles, smaller than cars
- For the 12. _____ roads in cities
- Got the name because of the 13. _____ sound
- No protection from breathing in the 14. _____ and gases
- Passengers must 15. _____a price with the driver before the ride

Water-taxi in Italy

- The fastest and most 16. _____ way to ride around the waterways
- Most local people cannot pay the price for the ride so they use 17. _____ instead
- Take passengers to 18. _____ places in the city

Boda-boda in Kampala

- Provide a fun ride around the town
- Not have to wait in traffic
- Criminals attack to 19. _____ the motorcycles
- The government in Uganda is thinking about 20. _____ boda-bodas completely

Exercise 10: Listen, Read and Speak

Listen to the recording and complete the sentences below with ONLY ONE WORD OR A NUMBER.

The Future of Cars [1]

1. Almost all of the cars today are powered by _____, like petrol, gasoline and diesel. But experts say this needs to change.

_____

1   https://www.tingclass.net/show-8483-246851-1.html

2. October 1, _____ marked that people could buy the Model T Ford, which was extremely popular.

3. One of the most popular ideas is to use hydrogen fuel cells that are stored in the car to create electric power because they release only _____ into the air.

4. These cars simply do not _____.

5. Using hydrogen is _____ to the environment, but making hydrogen is not so making hydrogen is costly.

6. Another way to power cars was using _____ but such cars were slower and could not travel as far.

7. Electric cars carry _____ to store the electricity.

8. One advantage of this is that people can repower them at _____.

9. However, they cannot go very far, and the batteries are _____.

10. But a number of car companies believe there is a future for electric cars. One chief engineer believes it is possible to make a _____ electric vehicle.

✺ IX. Listen and Understand the Culture

Exercise 11: Listen, Read and Speak

Why Do the British Drive on the Left [1]
英国人为何靠左行驶

Taking the left hand side in traffic is a habit that goes back hundreds of years, possibly as far as the ancient Greeks, Egyptians and Romans, but certainly to an era when people habitually carried swords when traveling. As around 85%-90% of humans are right-handed, passing on the right-hand side would leave carriage and cart drivers more open to attack from people coming the other way. Knights with lances, squires with knives, peasants with pitchforks, everyone had to be ready for a dust-up at a moment's notice, and that meant keeping to the left so you could get a good swing at your assailants.

靠左行驶的习惯可追溯到几百年前，大约远至古希腊、古埃及和古罗马时代，就是人们会佩带刀剑出行的时代。由于85%～90%的人都习惯使用右手，如果靠右行驶，四轮和二轮马车夫更容易受相反方向的攻击。执矛骑士、佩刀乡绅或者扛耙农夫，每个人都得随时准备面对突如其来的袭击，这意味着靠左行驶能在关键时刻给对手漂亮一击。

1　闫先凤 编：《听力密码：听见英国》，中国水利水电出版社，2019年：第144页

In 1773, the British Government introduced the General Highways Act, which encouraged people to drive on the left. The Highway Act of 1835 later reinforced this, making it the law of the land.

1773 年，英国政府首次颁布了《普通公路法》，鼓励人们靠左行驶。在随后 1835 年的《公路法》中再次强调了这一点。这样，靠左行驶就成了这片土地上的明文规定。

Everyone else kept left, but with increasing traffic on the roads in mainland Europe, this began to cause confusion, and slowly, over the course of the next hundred years or so, the European nations began to move over too.

不过在欧洲大陆，随着陆上交通工具的增加，靠左行开始给人带来困扰，所以在接下来的几百年里，欧洲国家也慢慢转为靠右行。

Also, this divergent approach occurred at a time when the British and the French were very busy colonizing the world. Every country occupied by the Brits—like Australia, New Zealand, India and the West Indies—kept to the left, and the ones occupied by France moved over to the right. The Americas were split, with the new arrivals from Britain, Holland, Spain and Portugal keeping to the left, and the French colonies insisting on the right.

而且，这种分歧发生在英法两国忙于在全球范围内开拓殖民地的时候。英国的殖民地，比如澳大利亚、新西兰、印度和西印度群岛继续保留靠左行驶的方式，而法国的殖民地则靠右行驶。美国则被一分为二，新来的英国、荷兰、西班牙和葡萄牙殖民者又保持靠左行驶，而法国殖民者坚持靠右走。

However, two vehicles were about to force this situation to change. In the late 1700s freight wagons (including the great Conestoga wagons) became more and more popular, particularly in America. These were pulled by a chain of horses, arranged in pairs. The best place to sit in order to control these mighty beasts was on the back of the left-hand horse at the back, so you could whip the others with your right hand. With the postilion driver in position, the best way for one wagon to pass another without accidentally banging wheels was the right hand side of the road. And where the wagons went, everyone else followed. So driving on the right became more common.

然而，新兴的两种交通工具改变了这种格局。18 世纪末期货运马车（包括康内斯托加式宽轮篷车）越来越流行，尤其是在美国。这类货车由并排的两列马匹牵引前行。控制这些"大力士"的最佳位置是左侧最后一匹马的后面，这样才可以用右手挥动马鞭控制其他的马匹。由于是左侧驭马，为了防止两辆交错的马车车轮不小心撞在一起，最好的方式就是靠右行驶。马车往哪走，人们就跟着往哪走，所以靠右行驶就变得越来越普遍。

And then the motor car arrived. While original designs for cars put the driver in the front and center of the vehicle, it wasn't long before the advantages of having the driver able to see down the middle of the road became clear. And in those countries where car manufacturing became an essential industry for export, right-hand-drive vehicles with the steering column on the left quickly became a worldwide norm, forcing relative latecomers like Sweden to give in and move over too.

接着出现了汽车。汽车最初的设计是安排驾驶员坐在车子的前中部分，不久人们就发现驾驶员要能观察到中间路况才能方便驾驶。在那些以汽车制造为重要出口产业的国家，靠右行驶的"左驾车"快速成为全球标准，迫使汽车业后起之秀——如瑞典——不得不做出改变。

Although it's interesting to note that this arrangement does favour the left-handed driver somewhat, as their dominant hand is the one that never leaves the steering wheel. A right-handed driver in a British car spends a good deal of their time steering with his or her right hand while fiddling with the gear stick with their left, which seems the safest way. This may account for the relative popularity of stick-shift gearboxes in British cars to this day.

有趣的是，这种安排确实很适合左撇子的习惯，这样他们的优势手，也就是左手，就可以不用离开方向盘了。一个惯用右手的司机要开一辆英式汽车就得花费很多时间习惯用右手操作方向盘同时用左手控制变速杆，这种方式不失为最安全的方法。这也解释了为何英式汽车至今仍偏爱手动变速器。

What have you learnt from this passage?

1. New words

_____

_____

_____

2. Summary

_____

_____

_____

3. Your opinion

_____

_____

_____

Sports

Objectives:

- to know the sports in Britain
- to learn about sports centres on and off campus
- to practice the listening skill of catching the adjectives
- to know the popular sports games in Britain
- to know the British Men's Loyalty to Football

I. Warm up

Exercise 1: Dictation of Words

1. _____   6. _____   11. _____   16. _____

2. _____   7. _____   12. _____   17. _____

3. _____   8. _____   13. _____   18. _____

4. _____   9. _____   14. _____   19. _____

5. _____   10. _____   15. _____   20. _____

II. Background Information—Sports in Britain[1]

Many international sports were introduced by the British who take their leisure time very seriously. There is widespread participation in sport in Britain.

➤ **Football** (or soccer, as it is colloquially called), the most popular sport in England as well as in Europe, has its traditional home in England where it was developed in the 19th century.

➤ The game **Rugby** was invented at Rugby School in Warwich shire in the early 19th century.

➤ **Cricket**, the most typically English of sports, has been in existence since the 16th century. On an international level, 5-day Cornhill Test Matches.

➤ Although **tennis** has been played for centuries, the modern game originated in England in late 19th. The main tournament is the annual Wimbledon fortnight, one of the 4 tennis Grand Slam tournaments (四大满贯网球锦标赛).

➤ There is a considerable following and participation of **athletics** in Britain. For example, the London Marathon, which takes place every spring.

➤ The home of **golf** is Scotland where the game has been played since the 17th century and naturally the oldest golf club in the world is there: The Honourable Company of Edinburgh Golfers. The most important national event is the Open Championship with the Walker Cup for amateurs and the Ryder Cup for professionals.

Part I Sports Center on Campus [2]

● Sports Centre in Cambridge University

Although the Sports Centre provides a hub for Sport at Cambridge University, anyone can become a member of our gym and use our facilities. You do not need a connection to the University and we have some competitive membership options available.

Opened in 2013, the University Sports Centre has a Gym, Strength & Conditioning room, Sports Hall, Squash and Fives courts, Studios and a Team Training Room used by international performance athletes. We offer a wide range of sports clubs and fitness classes for both members

---

1 https://mp.weixin.qq.com/s?__biz=MjM5NDYzNTM0MA==&mid=205890886&idx=2&sn=3d6d06604d6 ce74559a0f41a6f5691e5&chksm=2f35ce651842477364305ce7562b93f232de66885010615661d29fb90d08 bd45dbf40955cedb&scene=27

2 https://www.sport.cam.ac.uk/about-us

and casual users. Having top class facilities allows us to offer you one of the best gyms in Cambridge.

The Sports Service also maintains dedicated athletics and hockey facilities at Wilberforce Road Sports Ground, while cricket and tennis have their home at Fenner's, one of the country's most historic and iconic sports venues. A range of other club and college grounds are available across the city, catering to rugby, rowing, and many other sports besides.

Cambridge University is recognised as much for its illustrious sporting tradition as it is for its excellence in education, learning and research. Over the past 150 years, the University has been home to some of the world's greatest sportsmen and women, from Michael Atherton, to Emma Pooley, to a host of Olympians and Paralympians.

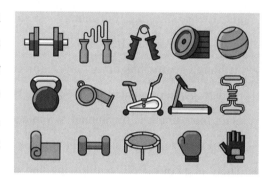

- Joining a gym in Cambridge

The University of Cambridge has one of the best gyms in Cambridge, open both to members of the University and the wider community. With a state-of-art Fitness Suite, Strength and Conditioning Room and Squash Courts, we will always have the right tools to deliver the workout you want.

We are also particularly proud of our staff. At the University of Cambridge Sports Centre, there will always be a friendly and experienced fitness professional on hand to cater to your needs—whether that be devising a personal programme, giving advice, or just having a chat. Our members testify that this is Cambridge's friendliest and most hands-on gym! We also run a range of classes, open to all of our members.

Whether you are a performance athlete training for a big event, or just someone wanting to use a treadmill at the weekends, we have a membership option to suit you.

- Cambridge Sport Membership

At the University of Cambridge Sports Centre, we want to offer our members more than just a gym. That's why we have introduced our new membership; Cambridge Sport. Being a Cambridge Sport member will allow you to fully embrace a healthy lifestyle involving a lot more than being a slave to a treadmill. Variety is the key to a successful workout plan and we believe Cambridge Sport allows you push yourself in more than just one direction.

Key Membership benefits include:

■ Access to both the Gym and Strength & Conditioning Room at any time we are open.

■ Personal Programmes designed by our highly qualified coaches

■ Inclusive access to our Fitness Classes*

■ Inclusive Badminton Court Hire*

■ Inclusive Squash Court Hire*

■ Inclusive Fives Court Hire*

■ Use of Wilberforce Road Athletics Track*

■ Inclusive access to Squash and Fives Play It Sessions

■ Free Equipment Hire for Squash, Fives and Badminton

■ Free Access to Workshops such as Barbell Club

*Subject to Availability, guest fees may apply.

We are pleased to offer this Membership with exceptional variety at very affordable prices. There is no minimum contract on our Direct Debit option but notice is required for cancellation. For further information, please see our **Terms & Conditions.**

Member Type	Monthly DD Membership	Annual Membership	Joining Fee
Community	£40	£440	£20
Staff, Alumni and Other Students	£35	£385	£20
University of Cambridge Students	£30	£240 Universal Membership £190 (Academic Year) £70 for 3 Months	£10 (paid by your college)

Part II The Gym Off Campus [1]

● About The Vault Gym

The Vault Gym is one of the largest personal training-only facilities in the country with a gym space of over 4,000 square feet, staffed by some of the industry's leading fitness professionals.

1　http://www.thevaultgym.com/about.html

➢ We charge no membership fees—the only fee you pay is for the time you spend with your trainer.

➢ We do not allow the gym to be used by non-clients, so you can enjoy a focused uninterrupted training session.

➢ We will take care of every aspect of your health and fitness lifestyle, designing you a bespoke fitness program that will enable our trainers to push you well beyond your own expectations and help you achieve your fitness goals.

➢ We will assess your diet for optimum weight loss or performance and correct any postural imbalances. We can rehabilitate form injury through our in-house clinicians and have a highly regarded referral scheme to many of the world's leading physiotherapists and doctors.

➢ We also provide a holistic approach to fitness though our specialised yoga and pilates instructors and we are one of the few gyms to offer a private studio for one-to-one practice.

➢ We also offer a home training service. This sees us send a trainer/yoga/pilates instructor or masseuse direct to your home or location

Whether it's your first step into fitness or you're being coached to perform at your best, it can be a challenging and demanding journey and we are here to help every step of the way.

- ## Our Services

Vault • Strong • Dedicated • Progressive • Passionate	At Vault, we have worked hard to get where we are today. Our dedication and application are driven by the desire to be the best in all that we do. Our team and unbeatable service are the embodiment of this ethic.
Elite Design & Consultancy • Inventive • Imaginative • Inspired • Precise	We take a good look at your space. Then we provide something truly inspirational. We consider practicality and functionality, but we consider the cutting edge too. A Vault gym design aims to take your fitness facilities to the highest level, to make them a success and to make them somewhere that people want to be—and want to return to.
Leisure Management • Exclusive • Innovative • Unique • Progressive	Five star facilities. High calibre gym equipment. Top level service. Your clientele deserve all this and more. So allow us to deliver it to them. On time, every time. Allowing Vault to manage and maintain your facilities gives you total peace of mind—and total success.

Continued

Pool & Spa Engineers ● Advise ● Clean ● Manage ● Service	Our superior pool, spa, sauna and steam room management services put you ahead of the pack. You deserve to be able to relax and unwind, just as your clientele do. By engaging Vault to deal with your pool and spa requirements, you put yourself in the best possible position to do exactly that. From design and management through to supplies and maintenance, we have it covered.

● **Personal Training**

The Vault Gym's personal training service is second to none. The PT team is over twenty-five strong and all of them are very well respected within the industry.

Many of the team have competed at an international level in their chosen sport, some have taken part in fitness competitions all over the world, while others have shared their knowledge and written books and articles for magazines, websites and newspapers.

We have many celebrity clients and the results of our training can be seen on the silver screen and in the music and television industry.

We treat every client as an individual and all sessions are tailor made to suit your needs and to help you achieve your goals.

We run a very friendly and unintimidating gym. It doesn't matter if you're new to exercise or a world champion, you will be made to feel welcome and comfortable from the moment you step through the doors.

Our trainers can help you lose or gain weight, train you for a sporting challenge, increase your fitness or help you to recover from an injury or illness.

As everyone's needs are different please contact us to answer any questions or concerns you may have and we will be happy to help.

- Boxing

The Vault Gym has its own dedicated boxing room. It's supremely well-equipped and has seen world champion fighters such as David Haye and Amir Khan training in the space.

Unlike many health clubs that offer boxing classes we have professional boxing coaches sanctioned by the British Boxing Board of Control.

We also have strong links to white-collar boxing organisations, should you want to face the ultimate challenge of going toe to toe in the ring.

III. Testing Key Points

　　运动场景通常发生在健身房（gym/fitness center/sports club）前台（reception），咨询办卡或会员信息。不同的俱乐部有各自的运动设施和课程设置，这是对话展开的一个中心内容。另一个重点展开内容就是对会员制度（membership scheme）、办卡流程（card application）以及各种课程（course/class information/ training session）的介绍。

　　不同的会员在设施使用、课程参加和费用交付上各不相同；办卡流程中需要留下各种个人信息。为了了解健身房的真实情况，可能会要求先做个身体评估（assessment）、上一堂试听课（trial session）、约定时间和教练等信息。

　　也有各种运动俱乐部的场景作为考点，比如足球俱乐部，此时考点涉及怎么加入俱乐部、申请者的个人信息、俱乐部的运动训练时间表、团体活动、各个负责人的名字和负责事宜、器材和设施的使用规定等。

IV. Word Bank

- Aquatics 水上运动

1. swimming 游泳

2. freestyle 自由泳

3. backstroke 仰泳

4. breaststroke 蛙泳

5. butterfly 蝶泳

6. medley 混合泳

7. water polo 水球

8. diving 跳水

● **Athletics 田径**

➢ Track 田径赛

1. 110m hurdles 110 米栏

2. 4×400m relay 4×400 米接力

➢ Jumping 跳跃

1. high jump 跳高

3. long jump 跳远

2. pole vault 撑竿跳高

4. triple jump 三级跳远

➢ Throwing 投掷

1. shot put 推铅球

3. hammer 掷链球

2. discus 掷铁饼

4. javelin 标枪

● **Road events 公路赛**

1. marathon 马拉松

2. walk 竞走

● **Ball Games 球类运动**

1. badminton 羽毛球

7. football 足球

2. men's /women's singles 男 / 女子单打

8. handball 手球

3. men's/ women's doubles 男 / 女子双打

9. hockey / field hockey 曲棍球

4. mixed doubles 混合双打

10. table tennis 乒乓球

5. baseball 棒球

11. tennis 网球

6. basketball 篮球

12. volleyball 排球

● **Cycling 自行车**

1. road cycling 公路自行车赛

3. points race 计分赛

2. track cycling 场地自行车赛

4. mountain bike 山地自行车赛

● **Equestrian 马术**

1. jumping 障碍赛

2. dressage 盛装舞步

● **Fencing 击剑**

1. foil 花剑

2. epee 重剑

3. sabre 佩剑

- Gymnastics 体操

1. artistic gymnastics 竞技体操

7. horizontal bar 单杠

2. floor exercises 自由体操

8. uneven bars 高低杠

3. pommel horse 鞍马

9. balance beam 平衡木

4. rings 吊环

10. rhythmic gymnastics 艺术体操

5. vault 跳马

11. gymnastics trampoline 蹦床

6. parallel bars 双杠

V. Basic Training

Exercise 2: Looking Around A Fitness Centre [1]

Answer the questions with NO MORE THAN THREE WORDS AND/OR A NUMBER and choose the best answer according to the recording.

1. Who shows the visitor around?

_____

2. Other than the toilets and showers, what facility is in the changing rooms?

_____

3. When does the weight training room open?

_____

4. What facility do the squash courts change into?

_____

5. What class is the club used for on Sundays mornings?

_____

6. Where can members find the schedule for the different classes?

_____

7. When is the club open?

A. Every day from 7:00 am

C. Every day from 11:30 am

B. Every weekday from 7:00 am

D. Every day from 7:00 am except Tuesday

---

1 上田真理砂 & Iain Davey 著，葛窈君 译：《听见英国——英式英语实境听力练习》，众文图书公司，2021 年：第 123 页

8. Before using the weight training room what must members do?

A. Learn how to use the equipment   C. Wear shorts

B. Take a short exam   D. Pay an extra fee

9. When can members take a special class in the swimming pool?

A. Between 10:00 am and 5:00 pm   C. At weekends

B. Between 7:00 am and 11:00 pm   D. Between 5:00 pm and 7:00 pm

10. When can't members take dance or aerobic classes?

A. Every day except Tuesdays   C. For two hours on Sundays

B. On Sundays before 10:00 am   D. Most days from 7:00 pm to 10:00 pm

Exercise 3 [1]

Listen to the recording to know about Olympic events and fill in the blanks.

1. _____ competed in Olympic events for the first time in _____ in 1900.

2. In _____, the first _____ Games were held in Chamonix.

3. In 1932, the first Olympic _____ was built to accommodate _____ in Los Angeles.

4. In _____ in Berlin TV _____ broadcast Olympic events for the first time.

5. The 1956 Olympics in _____ were the first Olympic Games to be held in the _____ hemisphere.

6. _____ hosted the first _____ Olympics in 1964.

7. In 1972 for the first time, over _____ TV viewers watched the _____ Olympic opening ceremony.

Exercise 4 [2]

Listen to the recording and complete the sentences below with ONE WORD AND/OR A NUMBER ONLY.

1. IOC governs the Olympics in general. It was founded in Paris on _____ 1894. Its headquarters are in the Swiss city of Lausanne. Its _____ languages are English and French.

INTERNATIONAL OLYMPIC COMMITTEE

---

1   http://www.kekenet.com/Article/201501/352061.shtml

2   https://www.tingclass.net/show-5753-14944-10.html

2. IOC members come from five different continents—_____, America, Asia, Europe and Oceania. They choose Olympic cities _____ in advance.

3. All the Olympic movements' _____ are contained in a book called *The Olympic Charter*.

4. There's an Olympic Museum and Studies Center in Lausanne. It contains _____, documents, medals, books, photos, paintings, films and _____.

5. The International Olympic Academy is a special center at Olympia in _____. People involved in sport go there every _____ to study the Olympic movement's _____, ideals and future.

Exercise 5

Listen to the recording and complete the summary below with ONE WORD ONLY.

Big Money, Better Game [1]

1. Foreign businessmen now own over half of the top football teams in 1. _____ from the owners without large 2. _____ resources although it will not bring them a 3. _____.

Roman Abramovich who made much of money from 4. _____ and invests in many different businesses. In 2003, Chelsea's owners had an increasing 5. _____ and Abramovich bought the team and wanted to help the players to be champions of Europe one day. His money brought a top 6. _____ to the club and many international football stars followed him there. In 2007, Chelsea reached the final of the European Champion's League which took place in 7. _____. Abramovich's investment has earned him 8. _____ in the international business world.

Traffic Sports is a company operating in 9. _____. It searches for young footballers and then 'buys' those players from their teams. Other teams in that country then pay to 'borrow' any one of these players to achieve better results. At the same time these young men can show how 10. _____ they are at football. This provides a way for major teams to discover new players to buy.

---

1   https://www.tingclass.net/show-8483-247097-1.html

VI. Listening Skill 7—Catching the Adjectives

听力考试中，形容词往往是最受青睐的出题点。为什么呢？这是从修饰的功能等角度来说的。一个句子最基本的结构是：主＋谓＋宾（当然也可以说主＋系＋表），句子最后核心部分或是核心意思一般由宾语（表语）体现，一个句子的表语或宾语大部分是名词（或词组）充当，而形容词在名词前往往被用来做修饰、做定语，所以在审题时需要重点关注形容词。因为名词很多时候以原文所给的信息出现，而形容词是最容易出现同义替换的，这是常见考点之一。

形容词在句中的位置大致有四种：①在名词前或名词后做定语；②在系动词后做表语；③在动宾结构后做宾语补足语；④独立结构，往往用于修饰主语的状态。

听力考试中，形容词的比较级和最高级也是值得注意的考点。

Practice

请同学们两两分组，老师分发两份不同的朗读段落，一个同学朗读一段文字，另一个同学把里面的**形容词**全部记录下来，然后检查核对。接下来，轮换进行。

_____

_____

_____

VII. Note-taking Practice

Exercise 6: Listen and Copy [1]

1. I'm so happy to finally get tickets to a soccer.

_____

2. Aston Villa is what we call a midtable team.

_____

3. Tickets aren't usually sold out.

_____

4. Next year I'll get a season ticket.

_____

1　米山明日香、Catherine Dickson 著：《英式英语听力 4 周大特训》，众文图书公司，2016 年：第 91 页

5. Are there any good seats left?

_____

6. You'll have a pretty good view of the pitch.

_____

7. I'm an Arsenal fan.

_____

8. Aston Villa is still winning 1-nil.

_____

Exercise 7: Listen and Write [1]

1. _____
2. _____
3. _____
4. _____
5. _____
6. _____
7. _____
8. _____

1　闫先凤 编：《听力密码：听见英国》，中国水利水电出版社，2019 年：第 65 页

VIII. Target Training

Exercise 8 [1]

Listen to the recording and fill in the blanks with NO MORE THAN TWO WORDS.

World Cup Football Players

For most football players, playing in the World Cup is a 1. _____. It is the result of hard work, practice, and many games.

Cyrille Domoraud from Ivory Coast played most of his career in Europe. In 2006, he played in the World Cup for his country and it was the 2. _____ moment of his football life. Due to this competition, the government in Ivory Coast became more peaceful. People lay down their weapons and work for peace.

Cyrille says that his Christian 3. _____ have been important to his football play. He also says that his Christian faith and his life in football are 4. _____ in some ways. Now he works with the Cyrille Domoraud Center, a training and 5. _____ center for young footballers.

Brazilian star Lucio thinks playing football has always given him great 6. _____. For him, playing for the 7. _____ team was very important and he is the 8._____ of the team.

He also thinks it important to create an environment of team 9. _____, order and discipline—encouraging his team-mates to have healthy 10. _____, speaking positively and encouraging them during the games, showing trust and acting professionally.

_____

1   http://www.tingroom.com/lesson/spotlight/162069.html

Exercise 9 [1]

Listen to the recording and complete the blanks below with ONE WORD AND/OR A NUMBER ONLY.

Finally, sportsmanship. It is an English 1. _____ and sport in this modern form is almost entirely a British 2. _____. Boxing, rugby, football, hockey, 3. _____ and cricket were all first organized and given rules in Britain.

Rules are the 4. _____ of sport, and sportsmanship is the ability to practice a sport on its rules, while also showing generosity to one's opponents and good temper in 5. _____. It is difficult to keep, but they are at least highly valued in Britain and are certainly achieved there more commonly than among more 6. _____ peoples.

Moreover, sportsmanship as an ideal is applied to life in general this is proved by the number of sporting terms used in ordinary 7. _____. Everybody talks of "fair play" and "playing the game" or "playing fair". Borrowed from boxing, "straight from the 8. _____" is used to describe a well-aimed, strong criticism and "below the 9. _____" is used to describe an unfair one. "Never hit a man when he's 10. _____" —in other words, never take advantage of a person's misfortune.

Exercise 10 [2]

Listen to the recording and complete the note below with ONE WORD OR A NUMBER ONLY.

Importance of Physical Activity

The WHO defines physical activity as "...any bodily movement produced by 1. _____ muscle that requires the use of energy."

The WHO encourage all people to do exercise 2. _____ days a week.

1　闫先凤 编：《听力密码：听见英国》，中国水利水电出版社，2019 年：第 164 页
2　https://www.tingclass.net/list-8483-1.html

This exercise should

- last for 3. _____ minutes.

- be 4. _____ intense.

- cause an increase in heart rate and 5. _____.

- cause a person to 6. _____.

Health benefits

- Muscles grow—and muscles are the parts of the body that control 7. _____ and assist in movement; give people more energy.

- Prevent some diseases in adults, including 8. _____, breast cancer, and type two (or 'adult') diabetes.

People not active enough

The WHO says that 9. _____ of the world's population does not do enough exercise.

Reasons for lack of movement

- People using 10. _____.

- Activities can be completed while 11. _____.

- Physical activity greatly decreased.

Extra problems

- Too crowded, too much 12. _____, too much crime, too much traffic, and too much air pollution.

- Too few 13. _____ spaces for exercise.

- Too few sports and recreation centers.

Two other reasons

- Too much costs.

　"Get a Life, Get Active" provides many ideas about how families and 14. _____ can include physical activity in their lives.

- Too busy or too 15. _____.

Exercise 11 [1]

Listen to the recording about the boat race between Cambridge University and Oxford University. Give short answers to the questions below with NO MORE THAN THREE WORDS AND/OR A NUMBER.

1. In which season will the Oxford University Boat Club and the Cambridge University Boat Club hold a rowing race on the Thames?

_____

2. What color are the members of Cambridge team traditionally dressed in?

_____

3. In which year was the tradition started?

_____

4. In which city did the Cambridge club prefer to hold the boat race?

_____

5. About how many people watch the race live from the banks of the river every year?

_____

6. How long is the game over?

_____

7. Which team wins more?

_____

8. When did the 2009 boat race take place?

_____

Tips:

每年复活节期间，英国牛津与剑桥两所世界顶级大学之间，都要在泰晤士河上进行一场"赛艇对决"（见图）。这是世界上历史最悠久的学校间赛艇对抗赛。近两百年来，这一传统竞技项目，每每让人热血沸腾。河岸两侧，观众多达30万，世界收看直播观众更是达到2 000万。

1829年6月10日，比赛在伦敦泰晤士河牛津郡的亨利段河面进行。牛津大学在首次比赛中获胜。比赛都以挑战形式进行，由上一年输

1　https://easylearn.baidu.com/edu-page/tiangong/questiondetail?id=1722654993440466976&fr=search

的队向赢的队发起下一年挑战，约定来年再赛。直到 1836 年，才举办第二次。最初 25 年里，比赛不定期举行，到 1855 年举行了 12 届。从 1856 年开始，除两次世界大战外，每年都如期举办，变成一个年度盛会。

Exercise 12 [1]

Listen to the recording and complete the note below with ONE WORD AND/OR A NUMBER ONLY.

Cliff Diving

- In cliff diving, the divers jump from the top of a cliff—from a 1. _____ edge of land, high above the water. Unlike other kinds of diving, the person enters the water 2. _____ first.

- Cliff Diving originated on the Island of Hawaii in 1770. The king of the island felt that this would prove their 3. _____ and loyalty.

- Today, there are around 4. _____ professional cliff divers around the world.

- Places to dive

- from the cliff edge

- from a 5. _____ over the water

- off bridges

- from high structures and dive into 6. _____

- Cliff diving is very dangerous

- jumps 18-28 metres

- moving speed at 7. _____ kilometres per hour

- 8. _____ are a common problem—divers could land on the rocks or they may be unable to swim through the large waves back to shore.

- Cliff divers are always looking for new diving places. The most famous cliff diving places are in Hawaii, Mexico, Jamaica, 9. _____ and Switzerland.

- Make sure you stay safe before diving

- Be careful about the 10. _____ you choose.

- Stay within your 11. _____.

- Throw a rock off the top and watch.

- Walk down to the water and swim around.

1　https://www.tingclass.net/list-8483-1.html

● Other tips:

- Never dive head first into water.

- Begin with a "12. _____ dive".

IX. Listen and Understand the Culture

Exercise 13: Listen, Read and Speak [1]

British Men's Loyalty to Football
英国男士对足球的钟爱

British men show far more loyalty, commitment, and self-sacrifice towards their favourite football team than towards their partner, a study showed.

一项调查显示，如果拿足球与伴侣相比的话，英国男人更加钟爱他们所支持的球队，他们对自己所支持的球队更加忠诚，更乐于承担义务，也更加富有牺牲精神。

Some 94 percent said they would never stop loving their team no matter how bad they were while 52 percent would gladly ditch a relationship that was not going well, the survey of approximately 3,000 men across Britain found.

在 3 000 名参加此项调查的英国男士中，约有 94% 的受访者表示，无论球队的成绩多么糟糕，他们都会继续支持自己所钟爱的球队。52% 的男人表示，如果与女友的关系发展得不顺利，他们不会像支持自己所钟爱的球队那样支持下去，而是会选择放弃。

Psychologist Aric Sigman said, "If men showed the same fidelity, commitment, self-sacrifice and honesty toward their partners, the divorce rate would halve overnight".

心理学家艾瑞克·西格曼说："如果男士能够像他们支持自己心爱的球队那样，对自己的伴侣表现出忠诚、诚实、投入和自我牺牲精神，那么英国的离婚率将会减少一半。"

In an age where politicians, loyalties are seen as chameleonic, where jobs and relationships come and go, loyalty is now reserved for something men feel they can actually believe in football.

人们正处于这样一个时代：政治家的赤诚之心像变色龙一样善变，工作和关系反复无常，在男人眼里，足球才是他们唯一可以百分之百信任的朋友。

---

1 闫先凤 编：《听力密码：听见英国》，中国水利水电出版社，2019 年：第 159 页

Perhaps this undying loyalty for a football team shows how qualities such as integrity and devotion are at a premium nowadays. A quarter of men admitted they would miss a family funeral to watch a game.

也许对于足球的忠诚之心证明了正直与牺牲自我精神在当今社会是多么难能可贵。近 25% 的英国男士承认他们宁愿放弃参加亲戚的葬礼，也不愿放弃去看一场足球比赛。

The research also discovered that 59 percent of Englishmen surveyed said football gave them a sense of national pride, while 55 percent of Scotland, embarrassment. The study also found that football provided a way for men to show emotion.

调查结果显示，59% 的英格兰男人认为足球赋予了他们民族自豪感，而 55% 的苏格兰男人却认为足球使他们产生了一种民族自卑感。调查同时发现，观看足球是男性宣泄情绪的一种方式。

Nearly two-fifths admitted they had cried tears of joy or despair over football whilst, almost a third said it had been crucial in teaching them to bond with other men.

近 40% 的受访者承认，他们曾经为足球流下过喜悦或伤心的泪水，近 33% 的男士认为足球能够促进男士之间的交流。

What have you learnt from this passage?

1. New words

_____

_____

2. Summary

_____

_____

3. Your opinion

_____

_____

Tips

英国足球流氓（hooligan）最为著名。足球流氓造成了许多足球场上的惨案。从 20 世纪 60 年代开始，英国足球流氓在全球范围内声名狼藉。英国国内媒体将其喻为"英格兰的灾难"。著名的海瑟尔惨案就是足球流氓的经典作为。1985 年 5 月 29 日，利物浦与尤文图斯在布鲁塞尔海瑟尔体育场的欧洲冠军杯决赛中相遇，欧足联赛前把一个球门后的看

台分配给利物浦球迷，但是有不少尤文图斯的球迷从比利时人手中买到该看台的球票。看台上，也没有足够的警察和工作人员将两队球迷分开。于是在比赛中，不断有双方球迷的辱骂和投掷行为。混在利物浦球迷中的足球流氓与尤文图斯球迷大打出手，导致看台倒塌，当场压死 39 名尤文图斯球迷，并有 300 多人受伤，这就是著名的"海瑟尔惨案"。而利物浦输掉了欧洲冠军杯决赛，赛后所有的英国球队被禁止参加欧洲的赛事长达 5 年之久，利物浦则长达 7 年。

Unit 8

Animals

Objectives:

- to learn about some animals in London Zoo
- to know the different body parts of animals
- to know some animals habits
- to practice the listening skill—catching other key words
- to know the different forms of negative expressions

 **I. Warm up**

Exercise 1: Dictation of Words

1. _____	6. _____	11. _____	16. _____
2. _____	7. _____	12. _____	17. _____
3. _____	8. _____	13. _____	18. _____
4. _____	9. _____	14. _____	19. _____
5. _____	10. _____	15. _____	20. _____

✿ II. Background Information— London Zoo [1]

London Zoo is one of the oldest zoos in the world. The garden was established on April 27, 1828. At first, the animals in the park were the research objects of scientists. It was opened to the public in 1847. More than 755 species and 15,000 animals were exhibited, with the largest collection in Britain.

● Penguin Beach

Penguin Beach recreates a South American beach landscape in the heart of London, with stunning colony of Humboldt penguins.

The exhibit features a large pool with stunning underwater viewing areas so you can see how our flippered friends fly under water. The exhibit's 1,200 sq. metre pool holds 450,000 litres of water!

Our large demonstration area turns feeding time in to an even bigger spectacle than before. Penguin Beach Live features twice daily feeds where visitors can watch the birds diving for their food.

Penguin Beach is a breeding facility for colonies of Humboldt penguins with a special penguin nursery, including a chick incubation unit and a pool where the youngsters can learn how to swim.

● Butterfly Paradise

Walking through a giant caterpillar, visitors are immersed into a world of amazing and beautiful butterflies and moths from around the globe. Lose yourself in the rich variety of species as they delicately flutter around you, seeking out plants on which to feed and rest.

London Zoo's Butterfly Paradise exhibit features species from several major regions including Africa, South-east Asia and Central and South America. Visitors can learn more about the conservation of this diverse insect group, from species recovery programmes, community-based habitat protection initiatives and climate change issues.

1　https://www.londonzoo.org/

Close up of butterfly with green and black markings in Butterfly Paradise. In 1981 ZSL London Zoo created the first exhibit developed exclusively for invertebrates. It featured mainly butterflies and moths—making it the world's first butterfly house!

Designed to resemble a giant caterpillar, Butterfly Paradise is a walk-through tropical haven, carefully planted and heated to a balmy 27 degrees to provide the perfect habitat for the beautiful invertebrates, which fly freely overhead in the exotic environment.

Butterfly Paradise itself was launched in May 2006 and it showcases a vast array of butterfly species in a carefully created 'walk though' environment, offering visitors the opportunity to learn more about life cycles, biodiversity and climate change.

Hundreds of butterflies have been chosen to represent 100,000 species that exist on the planet. All butterflies are forest-species from the shrinking tropics of South-East Asia, Central and South America and East Africa.

One of the most interesting aspects of Butterfly Paradise is the ever changing environment that is obvious not only in the development of the flora and fauna, but also in that it illustrates the entire lifecycle of a butterfly.

Highlights to look out for include tiny butterfly eggs, giant caterpillars and butterfly feeding stations.

III. Testing Key Points

雅思听力动物场景出现在 part 2 和 part 4 这两个部分中，尽管我们把这种场景归类于 part 4 的 Academic English 中，但在 Survival English 的 part 2 中也会出现，区别在于 part 2 重点描述的不是动物本身的特性，而仅是整个 zoo（动物园）导游过程的一部分，例如有个 part 2 主题是一个女人谈她参观 4 个 zoo 之后的感受，要求填写 rare lion 和 elephant 这两种动物。还有一个 part 2 主题是介绍一个 zoo 的布局，涉及动物的关键词汇是稀有动物的种类（species in rare animal area），包括 rare fish、goats, horses and hens，但新题有一个 part 2

主题为 wild zoo，部分内容与 part 4 的风格类似，考点有 red kangaroo（红袋鼠）的身高和 crocodile（鳄鱼）的寿命。

相对而言，雅思考试涉及的动物种类要少得多，其专业性也低得多。因此准备动物场景的第一个基本要求是对一些常见的动物名称熟练掌握，包括它们的发音、拼写以及最基本的生理特征和生活习性，特别是澳大利亚的一些最具特色的动物，例如 sheep, red kangaroo, koala, crocodile, dolphin, falcon, bat, ostrich，这些动物有的已经在雅思考试中出现过了，有的还未出现。掌握这些动物的基本知识，特别是中国很少见到的一些动物，有助于提高大家的听力理解能力。例如曾经考到的 red kangaroo（红袋鼠），就考到 it is higher than a person 的说法。

由于目前雅思听力场景中较少涉及动物方面，因此建议大家看一下 Discovery 有关动物方面的视频，其中就有雅思已经考过的动物。此外，有一档从英国引进的节目《玩转地球》，英国口音，中文字幕，对于练习听力以及掌握一些动物的习性也非常有好处。

IV. Word Bank

● 动物（陆地）

1. kangaroo 袋鼠	4. rhino 犀牛	7. hippos 河马
2. koala 树袋熊	5. ostrich 鸵鸟	8. crocodile 鳄鱼
3. snail 蜗牛	6. platypus 鸭嘴兽	9. kiwi 几维鸟

● 动物（海洋）

1. shark 鲨	4. tuna 金枪鱼	7. tortoise 海龟
2. dolphin 海豚	5. jellyfish 水母	8. squid 鱿鱼
3. whale 鲸	6. coral 珊瑚	9. salmon 三文鱼

● 动物（天空）

1. falcon 猎鹰	4. eagle 鹰	7. swan 天鹅
2. pigeon 鸽子	5. seagull 海鸥	8. flamingo 火烈鸟
3. owl 猫头鹰	6. parrot 鹦鹉	9. swallow 燕子

- 动物身体部位

1. head 头	8. back 背	15. fur 毛皮
2. eye 眼	9. body 身体	16. leg 腿
3. ear 耳朵	10. stomach 腹部	17. tail 尾巴
4. tongue 舌头	11. hair/mane 鬃毛	18. claw （尖）爪子
5. tooth 牙齿	12. skin 皮肤	19. paw 爪子，脚掌
6. beak 喙	13. leather 皮革	20. hoof 蹄
7. neck 颈	14. feather 羽毛	21. wing 翅膀

- 动物行为（animal behavior）

1. migrate 迁徙	4. hunt 捕猎	7. habitat 栖息地
2. mate 交配	5. feed 进食	8. predator 捕食者
3. breed 繁殖	6. hibernate 冬眠	9. prey 被捕食者

V. Basic Training

Exercise 2 [1]

Listen to the recording and complete the sentences below with ONLY ONE WORD.

War Pigeons

1. A pigeon can find its way back, even from a _____ place far away.

2. Experts believe that pigeons use the _____ and the earth's magnetic field to establish direction.

3. People raise pigeons in 'lofts' and race pigeons for _____.

4. At the beginning of World War Two, 7,000 of Britain's pigeon owners gave their pigeons to help carry _____.

5. During World War Two, British forces used nearly _____ birds to let the British air force know what had happened.

1　https://www.tingclass.net/show-8483-257733-1.html?gfh

6. Dickin Medal is for animals that have served humans in a special way when it is in _____ or conflict.

7. The PDSA provides health care for _____ animals.

8. The Dickin Medal was established in _____.

9. Altogether, PDSA has awarded _____ Dickin Medals to animals for their brave service during war.

10. The latest animal to receive it was a dog called Treo—for finding hidden _____ in Afghanistan.

Tips [1]

在战争期间，信鸽被配置到了一线作战部队，以便在电话和无线电通信无法联系时，与上级指挥部进行通信。有时这招还非常管用。

1943 年 11 月 18 日，对于信鸽吉杰来说是它一生中最伟大的时刻。信鸽吉杰仅用 20 分钟的时间便把消息传到了距离 40 英里外的一个指挥部，停止轰炸的命令最终在轰炸机即将起飞前送达，防止了村庄毁于轰炸，也避免了误炸友军事件的发生。

战争结束以后，1946 年信鸽吉杰被授予了玛利亚·迪肯奖章。这是英国专门为在战场上有着突出表现的动物设立的最高奖励。这枚奖章等同于人类世界里的维多利亚十字勋章。

Exercise 3

Part 1: Listen to the recording and complete the flowchart below with the ONLY ONE WORD you hear.

> The first cats came from the wild about 1. _____ years ago.

↓

> African wild cats in Egypt hunted and ate mice, rats, and 2. _____ .

↓

> The Egyptians were grateful and returned with small pieces of 3. _____ .

↓

_____

1　https://baijiahao.baidu.com/s?id=1622508860314113787&wfr=spider&for=pc

> The Egyptians looked after the wild cats.

↓

> The cats became the 4. _____ for Egyptians.

↓

> The image and shape of cats began to appear on jewellery and 5. _____.

Part 2: Listen to the recording and match the statements of beliefs or stories with different countries.

> A. It is good luck if a black cat walks in front of you.
>
> B. It is good luck to hear a cat sneezing.
>
> C. It is bad luck if you dream of a white cat.
>
> D. It is bad luck if you see a white cat at night.
>
> E. It is bad luck to carry a cat to go across a stream.
>
> F. It will be cold if a cat washes behind its ears.
>
> G. People will lose money if a cat leaves a house.
>
> H. Guests will come if a cat washes behind his ears.

6. Dutch   _____

7. Britain   _____

8. America   _____

9. France   _____

10. Italy   _____

Tips [1]

　　猫文化是英国的文化中不可或缺的一部分。而猫能作为英国文化元素的代表，自然也有着极为重要的地位，有史学家考证，在中世纪的欧洲，大多数人就已经爱猫如命了。英国，不仅仅是英国短毛猫的家乡，更是纯种猫的家乡这个概念诞生的地方。

　　英国的维多利亚女王、英国前首相丘吉尔、英国著名物理学家牛顿都是爱猫如命之人。

1　https://zhuanlan.zhihu.com/p/75436882

Exercise 4

Listen to the recording and choose the best answers.

1. How much of bird species have some scientists predicted to be in danger of dying off in recent 50 years?

A. 10%   B. 12%   C. 15%   D. 20%

2-4. What are causing the loss of bird habitat? Please choose THREE correct reasons.

A. cutting down trees   E. spraying pesticides

B. polluting the rivers   F. making noises

C. building cities and roads   G. changing climate

D. planting new farm land

5-6. The loss of bird habitat will have effects on birds. Which TWO are mentioned?

A. They can find new places to make their homes, nests.

B. They will be easily found and hunted.

C. They may not give birth to babies.

D. They can find some new food.

E. They will lose their usual protection.

7-8. Temperature change will have effects on birds' food. Which TWO are correct?

A. If the birds migrate too early, they can find some new food.

B. Birds with strong beaks eat open seeds and nuts.

C. Birds with long thin beaks can eat liquid from flowers.

D. Birds with long thin beaks can get food more easily than birds with strong beaks.

E. Birds with strong beaks eat less food than birds with long thin beaks.

9-10. Other things can also affect birds. Which TWO are not mentioned?

A. bright city light

B. dark clouds

C. long particular paths

D. large city buildings

E. glass windows

Tips [1]

知更鸟是英国的国鸟，这是一种食虫的益鸟，性情温顺、体态俏丽。英国人十分喜爱红胸知更鸟，尤为崇拜雄性红胸知更鸟对自己所建立的疆域负有巡察及保卫责任的本能。传说知更鸟与圣婴出世有关，又被称为"上帝之鸟"。

英国人无论到哪儿定居，心里总怀念着知更鸟，因而把一些外表大致相仿、其实种属迥异的鸟类也称为知更鸟。于是就出现了印度"知更"、北美"知更"和澳大利亚"知更"。一般说起知更鸟的意义都是指《是谁杀死了知更鸟》一书所表达的意思，即反对种族歧视！杀死没有犯罪的黑人就如杀死一只无辜的知更鸟。

Exercise 5 [2]

Listen to the recording and complete the note below with the ONLY ONE WORD you hear.

Caring for Whales

Whaling

- Whaling is a part of many 1. _____, including ancient ones.

- Many people killed whales for their skin, fat, meat, and 2. _____.

- Whales began to greatly decrease.

Blue whales

- the 3. _____ kind

- almost disappeared completely in 4. _____

- became a 5. _____ animal in 1966

- started acting 6. _____ in 2007

  - stopped near southern 7. _____ instead of the coast of the Americas

- rising 8. _____ decreases food supply for Blue whales

Grey whales

- almost as large as Blue whales

- also almost disappeared

- 2007 study showed Grey whales were once again in 9. _____

- global warming makes it difficult for Grey whales to find food and have 10. _____

---

1   https://www.gugong.net/wenhua/40097.html

2   https://www.tingclass.net/show-8483-242929-1.html

VI. Listening Skill 8—Catching Other Key Words

听力中抓关键词，经过对大量题目的分析，我们发现名词在其中占大多数，原因很简单：如果我们是命题者，为了准备四个选项或者填充题目，往往倾向于将原文的某些内容改写，名词由于难以被其他单词替代，所以很难被改写，这可以帮助考生把握最重要的信息，形容词和动词则分列二、三位。因此，在听的过程中，抓动词也很重要，尤其是实义动词，它在句中起到语意表达的关键作用，是一个句子不可缺少的部分。除此以外，数词和否定也是非常关键的信息点，往往也是考点，是答案所在（数词的练习见第 2 单元）。

否定往往通过以下方式呈现：

1. 直接否定

（1）否定副词—not, no, never, none, nobody, nothing, neither... nor..., nowhere, hardly, seldom, rarely, scarcely, barely 等

（2）否定形容词

① 本身为否定意义的形容词，如 little, few, bad, negative, boring

② 加否定前缀的形容词，如 unnecessary, dishonest, impatient, inexpensive, irregular, illegal

③ 加否定后缀的形容词，如 useless, tax-free, waterproof

（3）否定动词，如 fail, prevent, curb, forbid, ban, reduce, refuse, miss, escape 等

（4）否定介词，如 without, from, except/but, against, beyond, out of 等

（5）否定连词，如 before, unless 等

2. 间接否定

（1）too...to 太……而不能……

（2）more A than B （与其 B 不如 A）

（3）more than + 含有 can 的从句

（4）would rather do sth than do sth 宁愿（喜欢）……而不愿……

（5）prefer to do sth rather than do sth 宁愿（喜欢）……而不愿……

（6）... is the last thing/person I like 我最不喜欢……

3. 特殊情况

（1）双重否定，如 The songs never fail to make the children smile.

（2）否定转移，如 I don't think/believe/expect/imagine/hope he will pass the exam. 或 It doesn't look like/feel/seem/appear it's going to rain.

（3）特殊句型，如 not only/just...but also; not... until... 等

Practice

请同学们两两分组，老师分发两份不同的朗读段落，一个同学朗读一段文字，另一个同学把里面的**动词**都记录下来，然后检查核对。接下来，轮换进行。

_____

_____

_____

❧ VII. Note-taking Practice

Exercise 6: Listen and Copy [1]

1. Clownfish（小丑鱼） live in warm ocean water.

_____

2. They live in reefs. Reefs look like hard, thin rocks.

_____

3. But they are actually made by small animals called coral.

_____

4. Reefs are full of animals and fish.

_____

5. Clownfish live with anemones（海葵）in these reefs.

_____

6. Anemones are unusual animals. They look like plants.

_____

7. And they are usually very dangerous to other fish.

_____

8. They sting and kill small fish for food.

_____

Exercise 7: Listen and Write [2]

1. _____

2. _____

3. _____

_____

1   http://www.tingroom.com/print_169349.html

2   http://www.tingroom.com/print_172121.html

4. _____

5. _____

6. _____

7. _____

8. _____

✿ VIII. Target Training

Exercise 8: VOA Special Words and Their Stories [1]
Listen to the recording and match the idioms with the correct meanings.

1. something is for the birds

2. a bird's-eye view

3. birds of a feather flock together

4. killing two birds with one stone

5. the early bird catches the worm

6. travel as the crow flies

7. eat crow

8. for chicken feed

9. chicken-livered

10. chicken out

A. similar people become friends or do things together

B. admit a mistake or defeat

C. do two things by performing only one action

D. not go out alone

E. a person who gets up early in the morning for work has the best chance of success

F. worthless or not very interesting

G. go the most direct way

H. a general look at an area from above

I. a small amount of money

J. easily frightened

Tips:

1. raining cats and dogs /to rain cats and dogs 下了很大的雨 / 倾盆大雨 / 瓢泼大雨

2. the hair of the dog that bit you 一个人酩酊大醉之后，隔天早上用来解宿醉的一杯酒

3. let sleeping dogs lie 警告对方不要冒着可能引发不好局面的风险（不要自找麻烦、自讨苦吃），过去的事情就让它过去吧，不要再去揭伤疤

4. dog's breakfast / dog's dinner 杂乱无章，乱成一锅粥，一团混乱

5. dog days 夏天中最热的时期，相当于盛夏（三伏天）

6. yellow dog 卑鄙的人，懦夫

7. a lucky dog 幸运儿

1　https://www.chinavoa.com/show-526-128677-1.html

8. big dog 大人物

9. work like a dog 忙得像狗一样

Exercise 9 [1]

Listen to the recording and complete the note below with the ONLY ONE WORD OR A NUMBER you hear.

Save the Albatrosses

Albatrosses live in the Pacific area. Their main food is fish. They can fly long distances without rest.

Wandering Albatross

- the largest
- wingspread: over 1. _____ metres
- weight: nearly 10 kg

Breeding

- Albatrosses gather in 2. _____, large groups to protect the young birds.
- The female bird produces a single 3. _____ egg.
- Both male and female birds look after and 4. _____ the egg for two or three months.
- They will also share the responsibility of looking after their young.

Serious threat

- fishing, especially the longline fishing to catch 5. _____
- using a long line of 6. _____ fishing hooks which is 7. _____
- stretching for over 8. _____ km with thousands of hooks.
- catching the albatrosses in the longlines when they dive into the water for fish

RSPB

- Changes in the way people fish can help save the birds
  - for example, training fishermen in new fishing methods or attaching 9. _____ to the long fishing lines will help them to sink.
- Leaders from 10. _____ countries have signed an agreement "A-CAP" to save the birds.

1　https://www.tingclass.net/list-8483-1.html

Exercise 10 [1]

Listen to the recording and complete the note below with the only word or a number you hear.

Save the Butterfly

Monarch butterflies

- wings: bright 1. _____ and black with small white 2. _____ on the edge
- width: about 9-10 cm
- most live in 3. _____ America
- travel to 4. _____ to escape the cold season

Reasons for disappearing

- the loss of their natural resting place
  - only 12 5. _____ for them to gather every year
  - people enter 6. _____ and cut down the trees
- the loss of milkweed plants
  - 7. _____ development destroys milkweed and turns these natural spaces into houses, 8. _____, and roads
  - weed killer, made of strong 9. _____, is used to kill weeds in the farm

To save Monarch butterflies

- groups, like Monarch Watch, work to stop the 10. _____ of the butterflies
- people can plant milkweed

Exercise 11 [2]

Part 1: Listen to the recording and choose the best answer.

1. In the 1930's, what happened in Australia?

A. Sugar cane plants were sold not very well.

B. Sugar cane beetles were damaging much of the sugar cane.

C. Farmers used frogs to eat the sugar cane beetles.

1   https://www.tingclass.net/list-8483-1.html

2   https://www.tingclass.net/list-8483-1.html

2. Why toads couldn't solve the insect problem?

A. The toads could not reach the beetles even when the beetles are young.

B. The toads didn't eat the cane beetles.

C. The toad's skin contains poison to hurt the native plants.

3. Which statement below is true?

A. The cane toads were not the only invasive species in Australia for thousands of years.

B. The cane toads were first brought by European explorers.

C. The cane toads were the first invasive species in Australia.

Part 2: Complete the summary below according to the recording. Fill in each blank with the ONLY ONE WORD OR A NUMBER.

Today, Australia has over 4. _____ different invasive species. The invasive plants compete with native plants for resources and usually damage the balance in local areas. Invasive species usually spread to new areas because people bring them.

Invasive species travel in many ways. Insects can travel inside packages of fruit and 5. _____. People sometimes introduce or 6. _____ invasive plants. Today, more governments and groups are trying to protect against invasive species.

Governments use machines and 7. _____ to control invasive species. They inspect containers at country 8. _____ to prevent invasive species from entering. They use native species to fight against invasive species.

Here are seven easy ways that you can help fight against invasive species.

● Use native plants.

● Remove plants correctly.

● Help remove invasive species.

● Do not transport 9. _____, animals, or plants.

● Do not release pets into the 10. _____.

● Be careful what you move.

● And finally, tell others.

♣ IX. Listen and Understand the Culture

Exercise 12: Listen, Read and Speak

The Queen and Her Dogs
英女王和她的狗

The Queen devastated by loss of her last remaining corgi.
女王因失去仅存的柯基犬而伤心欲绝。

The Queen has been left heartbroken after the death of her last corgi, Willow, who was almost 15，was put to sleep at Windsor Castle on Sunday. The dog had a cancer related illness and the Queen did not want her beloved pet to suffer further. The death brings to an end a remarkable history between the Queen and corgis dating back more than eight decades.

上周日，在温莎城堡里，年近 15 岁的 Willow 被实施了安乐死。Willow 是女王最后一只柯基犬，它的离去让女王心痛不已。这只狗患有癌症相关的疾病，而女王不希望她心爱的宠物遭受进一步的痛苦。Willow 的离去也终结了女王与柯基犬之间长达 80 多年的美好故事。

Willow was the 14th generation descended from Susan a gift to the then Princess Elizabeth on her 18th birthday. But her heritage dates back even further, to 1933, when the Queen's father George the sixth, then Duke of York, introduced a corgi Dookie into the royal family.

Susan 是女王（当时还是伊丽莎白公主）18 岁时收到的生日礼物，而 Willow 是 Susan 的第 14 代直系后裔。但王室与柯基犬的联系却更为长久。1933 年，女王的父亲乔治六世（时为约克公爵），将一只名为 Dookie 的柯基犬带进王室。

Insiders say the Queen has been hit extremely hard by the loss of Willow who had become her most devoted companion accompanying her as she moved between her four royal homes. She has mourned every one of her corgis over the years but she has been more upset about Willows death than any of them says a Buckingham palace source. It is probably because Willow was the last link to her parents and a pastime that goes back to her own childhood. It really does feel like the end of an era. This is not however the end of the Queen's dog owning life.

知情人称女王因 Willow 的离去而伤心欲绝。Willow 是女王最忠诚的陪伴者，在她辗转于四所皇家住宅时陪伴左右。白金汉宫方面的消息称：多年来，女王一直在悼念她的每一只柯基犬，但都比不上 Willow 离世给她带来的冲击。这也许是因为，Willow 是她与父母最后的联系，也是一种能让她回到童年的消遣。这让人觉得像是一个时代的终结。但并不是女王养狗的终结。

She has two dorgis corgi dachshund crosses Vulcan and Candy, and last year she agreed to adopt a corgi Whisper after the death of his owner a former Sandringham gamekeeper. However the link with Willow who was pictured in the official portrait to mark the Queen's 90th birthday two years ago was a precious one. Willow represents a significant thread running through the Queen's life from her teenage years to her 90s, says a courtier.

她还有两只道吉犬（柯基犬和腊肠犬的串种）Vulcan 和 Candy。去年，桑德林汉姆庄园的前猎场看守去世后，女王同意收养他的柯基犬 Whisper。然而，女王与 Willow 之间的感情却是弥足珍贵的。两年前，Willow 被画进了庆祝女王 90 岁华诞的官方肖像画。一位大臣表示，Willow 代表着女王从年少岁月到 90 余岁华发苍苍的一条重要人生轨迹。

For many many years she bred and raised corgis and to think that the last one has now gone is something of a milestone. In 2015, it emerged that she had stopped breeding Pembroke Welsh Corgis because of fears that with younger dogs around her feet, she might trip over and hurt herself.

多年间，女王一直在饲养柯基犬。人们认为，最后一只柯基犬的离去无疑是一个里程碑式的时刻。2015 年，女王停止了王室中彭布鲁克威尔士柯基犬的繁育，因为担心更年轻活泼的小狗绕着女王的脚跑来跑去，可能会导致她绊倒受伤。

Her Majesty was still feeding and exercising Willow until the weekend when the dog's condition worsened. On Sunday afternoon the decision was taken to call a vet. She does not like seeing her dog suffer and she knows that sometimes putting a dog down is the kindest course of action although that doesn't make her loss any less says the source.

本周末，女王还在给 Willow 喂食并和它一起玩耍，直到狗的身体状况急转直下。周日下午，女王请来了兽医。有消息来源透漏，她不愿意再看到她的狗受苦，也知道有时安乐死是最仁慈的行为，尽管这样做也丝毫无法减轻她的损失。

One comforting fact was that Prince Philip recuperating from his hip replacement operation was able to be with her at Windsor. The death comes in a busy week for the Queen as she welcomes leaders to the Commonwealth Heads of Government Meeting in London but however preoccupied she is the Queen always finds time for her dogs. She likes to feed them herself with the finest cuts of meat and chicken as well as crumbling up treats from her own plate.

令人欣慰的是，从髋关节置换手术中恢复健康的菲利普亲王在温莎城堡中陪伴着女王。Willow 去世的一周中女王非常繁忙。她正在伦敦欢迎来参加英联邦政府首脑会的议领袖们。但不管她多么忙碌，女王总能找到时间照顾她的狗。她喜欢将最好的肉切碎喂它们，也喜欢从自己的盘子里挑出食物，撕碎后给它们吃。

Since 1945 she has had more than 30 corgis many of them direct descendants of Susan who's first puppies Sugar and Honey born in 1949 marked the beginning of a new royal dynasty. At one stage there were said to be thirteen corgis lolling in the Queen's private sitting-room and nipping the heels of food men, prime ministers and ladies in waiting.

自 1945 年以来，女王先后拥有过 30 多只柯基犬，其中许多是 Susan 的直系后代。Susan 的第一胎宝宝 Sugar 和 Honey 于 1949 年出生，标志着新王朝的开始。有人声称，一度有 13 只柯基犬在女王的私人起居室里玩耍，轻咬着喂食者、首相和在此等候的女士们的脚后跟。

What have you learnt from this passage?

1. New words

_____

_____

_____

2. Summary

_____

_____

_____

3. Your opinion

_____

_____

_____

Objectives:

● to know the healthcare in Britain

● to learn about National Health Service (NHS) on campus

● to learn about some important issues in health care

● to practice the listening skill of writing and speaking while listening

● to learn about the welfare system in Britain

 **I. Warm up**

Exercise 1: Dictation of Words

1. _____	6. _____	11. _____	16. _____
2. _____	7. _____	12. _____	17. _____
3. _____	8. _____	13. _____	18. _____
4. _____	9. _____	14. _____	19. _____
5. _____	10. _____	15. _____	20. _____

❧ II. Background Information—Health Care in Britain [1]

For those who don't know, the UK is a state that has one of the best Universal Healthcare Systems worldwide. The truth is that a lot of systems located in every corner of the world are based on this one. The healthcare system in the UK is called NHS or National Health Service.

In this post, we are going to provide you with everything you need to know about healthcare in the United Kingdom.

One of the great things that everyone loves about healthcare in the United Kingdom is the fact that the government allows almost everybody to have free access to different healthcare services. This is always true despite your personality. When you are in the UK, you will have peace of mind knowing that doctors will treat you the same way as how they treat other patients.

The healthcare system in the United Kingdom does not care about the amount of money you have in your pocket. On the other hand, one of the drawbacks of this system is that you still need to pay some amount through taxes. But don't worry since it is only a few amounts. The good thing here is that the tax rate that exists in the said country is on par with the countries that don't have a healthcare system. These two are something you should know about healthcare in the UK.

- Improve Public Health
- No Discrimination
- Widespread Accessibility
- Less Paperwork
- Generous System
- Full Coverage
- Promote Human Right
- Takes Time
- Long Waiting Time

(https://www.baidu.com/link?url=jGtfBPDyQsLxr2OZ_nIvtXJaahwFvvUAtcwKSiA7qG6cI6KN5 4eBnf2k_839D2wH&wd=&eqid=c6e650f800016a950000000462f465c0)

---

1   http://www.theyoungvictoria.uk

The National Health Service (NHS) is the UK's state healthcare system providing a wide range of services including appointments with a doctor and hospital treatment. You should register with a doctor as soon as possible after your arrival in Cambridge. Your College will be able to advise on this and may recommend a GP practice.

Student visa and immigration health surcharge

Those applying for a student visa and coming to the UK for 6 months or longer will be required to pay an immigration health surcharge as part of their visa application fee.

Students will be required to pay £470 per year for the duration the visa will be granted. If the leave includes part of a year that is 6 months or less, the amount payable for that year will be £235. If the leave includes part of a year that is more than 6 months, the full annual amount of £470 will be payable. Family members applying for a dependent visa will also be required to pay the surcharge. The immigration health surcharge is in addition to the visa application fee.

For students applying for entry clearance from overseas, the surcharge will apply to visas granted for more than 6 months. Those applying for further permission to stay in the UK will pay the surcharge regardless of the new visa length.

The immigration health surcharge will entitle students to access the NHS in the UK at no additional cost in the same way as a permanent UK resident. This includes at the Doctor's surgery (known as General Practitioner or GP), a Healthcare Centre or in a hospital. You may need to pay for dental and optical treatment as well as medicine prescribed by the doctor and collected from a pharmacy. There are also exceptions for particularly expensive discretionary treatments.

If your visa application is not successful, you will automatically be refunded the immigration surcharge (but not the visa application fee). The surcharge will not be partially refunded if you depart the UK earlier than the expiry of your visa. The surcharge is also not refunded if you do not use the NHS during your time in the UK.

EU and Swiss nationals and the Immigration Health Surcharge Reimbursement Scheme

Students from the EU and Switzerland studying full-time in the UK may be eligible for a full or partial refund of the immigration health surcharge paid with their visa application if they have a valid European Health Insurance Card (EHIC) issued in an EU country or Switzerland. These arrangements are in accordance with the terms of the EU-UK Trade and Cooperation Agreement and the Swiss Convention. Guidance about the Immigration Health Surcharge Reimbursement Scheme is provided on the government website. If you meet the criteria for a reimbursement, you should consider your circumstances carefully before applying to the scheme. In particular, you should take into consideration the information outlined in the guidance about whether you wish to work in the UK and the access to NHS healthcare in the UK with an EHIC.

Family members of students who meet the criteria may also be able to apply for reimbursement of the immigration health surcharge if they are in the UK on a visa, hold a valid EHIC and are not working, or intend to work, in the UK.

The scheme is currently not available to students from Norway, Iceland and Liechtenstein. Students from outside Europe are also not eligible for the scheme.

The Department for Health and Social Care, the UK government department responsible for policy on health and adult social care matters in England, has produced an information pack for students which includes 'frequently asked questions' about the scheme.

Short study periods

If you apply for your visa from overseas and it is granted for less than six months or you are required to make a number of occasional visits to the UK for short study periods, you are advised to take out medical insurance as you will be liable for NHS charges for the treatment you receive in the UK except for in a medical emergency and this is limited. Some countries have a reciprocal agreement with the UK which may entitle you to some free healthcare on the NHS but you should seek advice from the health authorities in your home country about what treatment will be covered. EEA nationals should obtain a European Health Insurance Card (EHIC).

(https://www.baidu.com/link?url=3EmW7ciymc9xFYGEqBBIKkn6dew-1l8C9GJK5RRpXlOM8V UnY9pd3bA1aPJ2xTVOswVv5S-VXIeCpghSkyclklnvNtpgtcfTk0n-b-rt8n_&wd=&eqid=c6e650f 800016a950000000462f465c0)

III. Testing Key Points

　　健康医疗场景通常发生在诊所（clinic）和医院（hospital）前台 (reception)、咨询医生、介绍专业性讲座或课程等，这是对话展开的一个中心内容。

　　不同的医生擅长的领域不同，所以适合的病人也不同，常见的考点有：诊所医院的名称、地址、预约或看诊时间、擅长的病症、适合的病人（年龄）以及诊所会举办的讲座（名称、时间、举办地点、讲座主要内容、适合哪些人群来听）等。

IV. Word Bank

1. skin cancer 皮肤癌

2. (be) vulnerable to illness 容易生病的

3. stress-related illness 和压力有关的疾病

4. viruses and infections 病毒和感染

5. pharmacy 制药业

6. incurable/curable （不）可治疗的

7. circulation of blood 血液循环

8. immune system 免疫系统

9. inflammation 发炎

10. surgery/surgeon 外科手术 / 外科医生

11. cell-destroying 破坏细胞

12. traditional/conventional medicine 传统药物

13. welfare 福利

14. diet-related problems 饮食相关问题

15. symptoms of illness 疾病症状

16. disorder 混乱

17. cure 治愈

18. treatment 治疗

19. private healthcare 私人医疗

20. pills/tablets 药丸 / 药片

21. arthritis illnesses 关节炎和疾病

22. common illness 常见病

23. nutrient/nutritious 营养 / 营养

24. dietitian 营养师

25. ingredients 成分

26. overeating 暴饮暴食

27. protein 蛋白质

28. appetite 食欲

29. food allergy/be allergic to 食物过敏

30. infection 传染

31. unhealthy additives 不健康添加剂

32. vitamins and minerals 维生素和矿物质

33. overweight 超重

34. diagnose/diagnosis 诊断 / 诊断

35. psychological/physical 心理 / 生理

36. depression 抑郁症

37. hormones 激素

38. chronic disease 慢性病

39. muscle contraction 肌肉收缩

40. sleep disturbance 睡眠障碍

41. insomnia 失眠症

42. therapy/therapist 治疗 / 治疗师

43. staple diet 主食

V. Basic Training

Exercise 2 [1]

Listen to the recording and complete the note below with NO MORE THAN TWO WORDS.

Body Clock

Research shows that our bodies have their own rhythms

- to help people know

● when to get up in the morning

● when to eat

● when to go to bed.

Scientists believe that body rhythms repeat every twenty-four hours

and eleven minutes, almost the same length as a day!

---

1   https://www.tingclass.net/show-8483-242433-1.html

How does the body's clock work?

- SCN in the brain controls the body's clock.

It commands other organs and systems in the body to make everything work together. e.g.

- in the morning 1. _____ rises

- in the afternoon and evening, 2. _____ produces special chemicals to make you feel hungry

- at night, a gland in the brain starts to work.

- Melatonin makes you feel 3. _____.

- As you sleep, the 4. _____ in your body drops.

- In the morning, your body reduces producing melatonin.

The body clock is important for health

- Obeying your body's clock can help reduce tiredness and reduce the risks of being obese, or over a normal weight.

- Changing your body's 5. _____ can cause serious health problems.

Exercise 3 [1]

Part 1: Listen to the recording and choose the best answer.

1. Sleeping sickness is a disease passed on to humans by _____.

A. dogs   B. birds   C. insects

2. People with sleeping sickness _____.

A. may increase weight

B. may become angry without any reason

C. may be difficult in working

3. Sleeping Sickness affects people only in _____.

A. South Africa   B. Sub–Saharan Africa   C. Ethiopia, Zimbabwe and the Congo

4. A WHO study showed that the disease affected _____.

A. 27,000 people   B. 30,000 people   C. 300,000 people

---

1   https://www.tingclass.net/show-8483-242437-1.html

Part 2: Listen to the next recording to complete the summary below with THE ONLY WORD you hear.

How to Deal with Sleeping Sickness

Sleeping sickness can be prevented. A person must wear 5. _____ clothes to avoid the disease which are not bright colored. It is important to look for the flies inside a 6. _____ before entering. And finally, people should sleep under a 7. _____. In Kenya, researchers are reducing the fly population by using 8. _____.

But what can a person do if an infected fly does bite them? Knowing about the disease is the first step in getting treatment instead of thinking the person has an 9. _____ spirit. People should go to see the doctor. But most people do not know that they are sick until they are in the 10. _____ stage which is more difficult to treat. In this stage, doctors usually use Melarsoprol to treat the patients.

Exercise 4 [1]

Listen to the recording to complete the note below with THE ONLY WORD you hear.

Washing Hands Works

Germ Theory of Disease

Avoiding or killing germs is the best way to avoid 1. _____.

- In a health care situation it is best to kill germs with 2. _____ soap.
- Sadly, hand washing may just seem difficult for health 3. _____ workers.

---

1   https://www.tingclass.net/show-8483-243309-1.html

A Study

- fIn all, the researchers studied over 4. _____ households

• with at least two children younger than fifteen.

• at least one child younger than five.

- Living conditions for each family were similar:

• Most families had a toilet.

• Families could usually easily get soap for a good 5. _____.

• Many people wash their hands with only water for 6. _____ ceremony.

• Washing hands was not a common every day.

- Three family groups:

• One group received a supply of powerful 7. _____ soap.

• Another group received a supply of 8. _____ soap.

• The control group did not receive any soap from the researchers.

Conclusions:

• The health of families in the control group did not change. Children in these families who received soap and hand washing education had 9. _____ fewer cases of diarrhea.

• Babies in these families had 10. _____ fewer days of diarrhea.

• These results were similar in the two groups with soaps.

Exercise 5 [1]

Listen to the recording and complete the summary below with ONE WORD ONLY.

Caring for the Heart

1. The heart beats _____ in one's life

A. over 500 million times

C. over 2,250 million times

B. over 2,000 million times

D. over 2,500 million times

---

1   https://www.tingclass.net/list-8483-1.html

2. The heart pumps over _____ of blood each day and send blood around the body.

A. 3,000 liter   B. 6,000 liter   C. 7,000 liter   D. 17,000 liter

3. Every year over _____ people die from CVDs.

A. seven   B. seventeen   C. seventy   D. seven hundred

4. There are several risk factors that can lead to heart disease, which of the following is **NOT INCLUDED**?

A. An unbalanced eating   C. A lack of exercise

B. A lack of sleep   D. Tobacco smoking

5. In the United Kingdom, a government programme reduced the amount of salt in around _____ of processed foods.

A. 5%   B. 15%   C. 25%   D. 35%

6. Which one is **NOT** the characteristics of the traditional Korean diet?

A. Low in fat   C. Using traditional cooking methods

B. Containing lots of vegetables   D. Spicy food

7. In Mauritius, the government led a project to change the oil that people cook with _____.

A. palm oil   B. bean oil   C. soya bean oil   D. vegetable oil

8. Indians try to avoid milk fats like butter because _____.

A. all of these are high in bad fats   C. they will cause high blood pressure

B. they will lead to heart disease   D. they will lead to overweight

9. Which one is **NOT INCLUDED** in the experts' advice?

A. Avoid oil cooking   C. Avoid smoking.

B. Avoid sleeping late   D. Avoid too much red meat

10. World Heart Day is _____.

A. the last Saturday of September   C the last Saturday of December

B. the last Sunday of September   D the last Sunday of December

VI. Listening Skill 9—Listen, Write and Speak

虽然大家都会觉得这是非常好的方法，受益颇多，但鲜少有人去坚持做，做的人当中也鲜少有人能够成功。做听力的过程中，很多人会发现：题看不过来，裸听也听不懂。做题的技巧是套路性的东西，但"裸听"就是实打实的能力了。套路可以一点就通，能力却只能靠量变到质变。

"听抄、听写和跟读的全过程"

第一步：通听一遍

要点：

1. 有题的话可以先做一遍题，要是没有，就裸听

2. 裸听，记下尽量多的信息和疑惑点

第二步：逐句写下（听抄的核心环节，但不是最重要环节），大家可去找一个合适的App，能单句播放为佳

要点：

1. 每一句，先听懂然后再写。不要听一个单词写一个单词

2. 如果你发现你就算听懂了也不能原样写下来，那就对了，这就是因为你的语言运用功底不够，或者记性不如想象的那么好，因此，在做听力题的时候很可能因此失分

3. 但练习听抄能很好地摆脱这一点

4. 不要过多纠结这一句，尽量快地把这个section写完

5. 标注好没听清的或者有发现的地方

（第一次听是真实水平的反映，反复听之后会导致越听越清楚，但听不懂的连读和语言现象仍然没引起你的重视。这就非常不好了，所以一定要标注好初听的疑惑处）

第三步：再一句一句听一遍（基础较好的考生可以把这一步放到第二步一起做）

要点：

1. 不看原文，只是相当于再给自己一次机会更正答案

2. 千万不可跳过这一步，具体原因见下一条

3. 注意语言现象，如连读和辅音浊化现象，以及之前勾画出的没听懂的单词、连词甚至句子。一定要引起足够重视！

4. 标注出来，这一步很重要，因为可以帮助你找出自己最大的问题。大多数人主要的问题是在连读和发音上。事实上，如"percent of"这个节段，native speaker 不会 percent of 这

样发音，他们只会读成"percen-tof"这样。

第四步：核对原文，修改答案

核对原文，然后统一总结失误（心里总结也可以，但好记性不如烂笔头）

错误大致分为三类。

1. 连读，是错误最多的一类

2. 生词，需要积累

3. 英式发音总结和习惯。

第五步：跟读与裸听

要点：

1. 特别注意之前的标注点，纠正自己发音

2. 学习原材料的发音、语调、速度和语言使用方法

3. 反复练习直到你的发音速度和原文一样

4. 然后盲听，不看材料，跟读

5. 裸听，不跟读，看自己能不能把每个点都听清楚。

6. 速度调到 1.2 倍、1.5 倍，甚至 2 倍，通过加快语速，刺激自己的反应速度

第六步：找一篇相似的材料，裸听

这一步不用做听抄，只是作为对上一篇听抄的一个反馈和巩固，真正能力的提升也就在这里。

VII. Note-taking Practice

Exercise 6: Listen and Copy [1]

1. Polio（小儿麻痹症）is a very serious disease. It is often spread by infected human waste.

_____

2. Usually, people become sick with polio after drinking or touching dirty water or waste.

_____

1　https://www.tingclass.net/list-8483-1.html

3. Many children become infected by swimming in infected water.

_____

4. Polio affects a person's nerves. It can make a person unable to move.

_____

5. In the worst cases, a person may not be able to breathe.

_____

6. Polio was a big concern in the United States and Europe in the 1940's and 1950's.

_____

7. Many people became sick every summer. These epidemics were getting worse.

_____

8. Many scientists had tried to develop vaccines, but none were successful.

_____

Exercise 7: Listen and Write [1]

1. _____

2. _____

3. _____

4. _____

5. _____

6. _____

7. _____

8. _____

9. _____

_____

1   https://www.tingclass.net/list-8483-1.html

VIII. Target Training

Exercise 8 [1]

Listen to the recording and fill in the note with ONLY ONE WORD.

Obesity in children is a growing problem everywhere like Latin America, Asia, even 1. _____.

Negative effect

Obese diabetic children are more likely to:

- develop other diseases when they are adult
- be unable to work, which will put pressure on their national 2. _____.

A healthy body will:

- change foods into a simple 3. _____, then it moves into the blood.
- produce insulin（胰岛素）which helps the glucose（葡萄糖）move from the blood into 4. _____.
- then use the glucose for 5. _____, or store it.

Two types of diabetes

- Type one is when the body system wrongly attacks the cells that make the insulin.
- Type two is among about 6. _____ of people with diabetes.

In most cases type two diabetes is linked to being 7. _____.

To avoid obesity and diabetes

- Parents can 8. _____ their children to make the best food choices.
- IDF and World Health Assembly advise:
- Healthy diets at an early age.
- 9. _____ food information on products.
- More sports and physical activity.
- Less 10. _____ effects of unhealthy food on children.

---

1   https://www.tingclass.net/list-8483-1.html

Exercise 9 [1]

Listen to the recording and complete the note below with the ONLY WORD you hear.

Stop Smoking

Tobacco contains nicotine which is an 1. _____ substance.

There are many good reasons to stop smoking.

- First, smoking reduces a person's ability to 2. _____.
- Second, Smokers are more likely to get more serious diseases, like 3. _____ in the lungs and emphysema（肺气肿）.
- Third, cigarette smoke is harmful to the people around, especially 4. _____.

To stop smoking, there are many methods and treatments to try.

- Some people use Nicotine 5. _____ treatments to substitute cigarettes.
- Some people attend support groups to get encouragement.
- And other people also stop smoking just by counting how much money they 6. _____ if they stop buying cigarettes.

No matter which method is used, a smoker should always have a 7. _____, called START, which is:

- S—Set a 8. _____.
- T—Tell the people around you to get support.
- A—Anticipate or expect the difficulties.
- R—9. _____ cigarettes and other tobacco products.
- T—Talk to your doctor to get good 10. _____.

---

1   https://www.tingclass.net/show-8483-251578-1.html

Exercise 10 [1]

Listen to the recording of Art Therapy and choose the best answer.

1-3. In a festival for disabled youth in Iran, which **THREE** statements are true?

A. The festival is held every year in Iran.

B. There are only a few skilled performers.

C. Only one team will get an award for the 'best act.'

D. There are several creative acts from other nations.

E. Not all of the performers have some kind of disability.

F. They have a strong competition.

G. All of the performers are under 20 years old.

4. Hatef Doostar thinks that art therapy is closely related to _____.

A. music   B. colour   C. culture

5. Hatef Doostar teaches young disabled people _____.

A. creative skills

B. acting skills

C. how to play musical instruments

6. A man who watched the festival _____.

A. was a disabled person himself

B. changed his views on disabled people

C. had tears for the wonderful performance

7-8. Hatef Doostar works in different places across Tehran. Which **TWO** statements are right?

A. He treats the patients with art, colour and communication.

B. He works for patients with three kinds of severe mental conditions.

C. He gets all the patients to sit in a circle.

D. The patients will dance to the music.

E. He brings new life into the hospital.

---

1   https://www.tingclass.net/list-8483-1.html

9-10. Which **TWO** statements about Doctor Aflatoonie are right?

A. He specialises in mental sicknesses.

B. He works at the same Hospital as Hatef does.

C. He disagrees on Hatef's work.

D. He supports that medicine creates a solution for everyone.

E. He believes that music therapy has some help but not that much.

Exercise 11 [1]

Listen to the recording and complete the note below with the ONLY WORD you hear.

Crying for Health

Three different kinds of tears

- basal tears

● keep our eyes 1. _____

● help our eyelids move

● help our eyes fight diseases

- reflex tears

● result when a foreign particle enters our eye

● help to 2. _____ the eye—removing dirt, dust and other bad things

- emotional tears

● Many emotions make people cry—including joy, sadness, anger, conflict, 3. _____, failure and success.

● People also cry when they experience physical 4. _____.

Why our emotions produce tears

- Crying protects our body

● the body produces particular substances like hormones and 5. _____ so crying can help people feel 6. _____

---

1   https://www.tingclass.net/show-8483-260461-1.html

- The crying club started in 7. _____. People gather together to help each other cry, like:

watching sad films

listening to sad music

cutting up 8. _____

- Crying is also 9. _____

- People in some cultures cry much more often than people in other cultures.

- In some cultures, people easily cry in public.

- But in other cultures, crying causes people to feel 10. _____.

IX. Listen and Understand the Culture

Exercise 12: Listen, Read and Speak

A Welfare State [1]
福利国家

Britain is regarded as a welfare state. This system is funded out of national insurance contributions and taxation. In Britain the term applies mainly to the National Health Service (NHS), national insurance and social security.

英国被认为是福利制度的国家。此制度所需的资金来源于全国保险税和赋税。在英国，这主要是指国民保健制度、国民保险和社会保障制度。

The National Health Service provides for every resident, regardless of income, a full range of medical services. The service was established in the U.K. in 1948. Over 82 percent of the cost of the health service in Great Britain is funded out of general taxation. The rest is met from: (1) the NHS element of National Insurance contributions; (2) charges towards the cost of certain items such as drugs prescribed by family doctors, and general dental treatment; (3) other receipts, including land sales and the proceeds of income generation schemes.

不管个人收入如何，国民保健制度为每个居民提供全面医疗服务。英国于 1948 年确立此制度。英国国民保健制度 82% 以上的费用来自普通税收，其他部分来自：（1）国民保健

1　闫先凤 编：《听力密码：听见英国》，中国水利水电出版社，2019 年：第 156 页

制度中的国民保险金部分；（2）某项医疗费用比如家庭医生开的药单和普通牙科治疗所收的费用；（3）其他收入，包括出售土地和创收计划的收益。

There are proportional charges for most types of NHS dental treatment, including examinations. Sight test are free to children. No one is liable to be charged by the National Health Service for treatment in an accident, emergency or for an infectious disease. Central government is directly responsible for the NHS, which is administered by a range of local health authorities and health boards throughout the U.K.

国民保健制度中多数牙科治疗要收取一定比例的费用，包括检查费。视力检查对儿童免费。国民保健制度对事故、急诊或传染病的治疗不收费，中央政府直接负责国民保健制度，由全国各地的保健机构和卫生委员会实施。

The family health services are those given to patients by doctors, dentists, opticians and pharmacists order to obtain the benefits of the NHS a person must normally be registered on the list of a general practitioner（GP, sometimes knows as a "family doctor"）.

家庭保健服务由医生、牙医、眼科大夫和药剂师提供给病人。为获得国民保健制度的服务，人们必须在普通开业医生（GP，有时候也被称为"家庭医生"）的名册上注册。

A full range of hospital services is provided by district general hospital. There are also specialist hospitals or units for children, people suffering from mental illness, those with learning disabilities, and elderly people, and for the treatment of specific diseases.

地区普通医院提供全面的医院服务。也有为儿童、精神病人、有学习障碍者、老人和特殊病人开设的专门医院或病区。

The National Health Service is the largest single employer of labour in the U.K. NHS has suffered from underfunding in recent decades, as a result of which many better-off people have been turning to private medical health care.

国民保健制度是英国最大的单一雇主，近几十年来，正遭受资金不足的困扰。原因是许多富裕的人正逐渐转向私人的医疗保健机构。

The social security system is designed to secure a basic standard of living for people in financial need. Nearly a third of government expenditure is devoted to the social security programme which provides financial help for people who are elderly, sick, disabled, unemployed, widowed, bringing up children or on very low incomes.

社会保险制度设立的目的是保障经济困难的人们的基本生活水平，政府开支的近三分之一用于社会保险计划。此计划给老人、病人、残疾人、失业者、寡妇、抚育幼儿者或低收入者提供经济帮助。

Administration in Great Britain is handled by separate executive s agencies of the Department of Social Security. In Northern Ireland by the Social Security Agency.

大不列颠的社会保险由社会保险部独立执行机构管理，在北爱尔兰则是社会保险局。

What have you learnt from this passage?

1. New words

_____

_____

_____

2. Summary

_____

_____

_____

3. Your opinion

_____

_____

_____

Education

Objectives:

- to know the famous universities in the world
- to know the importance of education
- to know some learning theories and techniques
- to learn about the listening skill—extensive listening and intensive listening
- to know the education system in UK

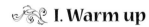 **I. Warm up**

Exercise 1: Dictation of Words

1. _____	6. _____	11. _____	16. _____
2. _____	7. _____	12. _____	17. _____
3. _____	8. _____	13. _____	18. _____
4. _____	9. _____	14. _____	19. _____
5. _____	10. _____	15. _____	20. _____

II. Background Information—University of Oxford in UK[1]

The University of Oxford is the oldest university in Britain and one of the world's most famous institutions of higher learning, established during the 1100s. It is located in Oxford, England, about 80 kilometers northwest of London.

牛津大学是英国最古老的大学，也是世界上最著名的高等学府之一，始建于 1100 年代。它位于英国牛津，在伦敦西北约 80 公里处。

Oxford is very competitive: more than 19,000 people applied for around 3,200 undergraduate places for entry in 2016, which means that Oxford receives, on average, nearly 6 applications for each available place. 40% of the total student body—over 9,300 students—is citizens of foreign countries. Students come to Oxford from over 140 countries and territories. There are 38 Oxford colleges plus six permanent private halls, which are similar to colleges except that they tend to be smaller, and were founded by various religious groups.

牛津大学的竞争非常激烈：2016 年有超过 19 000 人申请了约 3 200 个本科入学名额，这意味着牛津大学平均每个入学名额都会收到近 6 份申请。学生总数的 40%——9 300 多名学生——是外国公民。来自 140 多个国家和地区的学生来到牛津。牛津大学共有 38 个学院，外加 6 个永久性的私人大学堂，它们与大学相似，只不过规模较小，而且是由不同的宗教团体创立的。

At Oxford, each college is a corporate body distinct from the university and is governed by its own head and fellows. Most fellows are college instructors called tutors, and the rest are university professors and lecturers. Each college manages its own buildings and property, elects its own fellows, and selects and admits its own undergraduate students. The university provides some libraries, laboratories, and other facilities, but the colleges take primary responsibility for the teaching and well-being of their students.

牛津的每个学院都是独立于大学的实体，由该学院的院长和管委会成员负责管理。绝大多数管委会成员都是被称为导师的学院教师，其余的是大学教授和讲师。每个学院管理自己的房产和资产，选举自己的管委会，遴选和招收自己的本科生。大学提供一些图书馆、实验室和其他设施，但教学和学生生活主要由各学院负责。

1　https://www.360docs.net/doc/86906481.html

The university, not the individual colleges, grants degrees. The first degree in the arts or sciences is the Bachelor of Arts with honors. Oxford also grants higher degrees, diplomas, and certificates in a wide variety of subjects.

学位由大学而不是各个学院授予。文理科第一学位是优等文学学士。牛津还在其他众多学科领域授予更高的学位、文凭和证书。

Each student at Oxford is assigned to a tutor, who supervises the student's program of study, primarily through tutorials. Tutorials are weekly meetings of one or two students with their tutor. Students may see other tutors for specialized instruction. They may also attend lectures given by university teachers. Students choose which lectures to attend on the basis of their own special interests and on the advice of their tutors.

牛津大学给每个学生指定一名导师，主要通过辅导监督学生的学习。辅导课是一两名学生每周与导师的会面。学生如需专业指导，还可以去约见其他导师，也可以选听大学教师讲授的课程。学生选听什么课程是根据自己的兴趣和导师的建议而定的。

III. Testing Key Points

雅思听力考试中，教育场景一般出现在 part 3 中，往往是学生对课程的咨询 (course inquiry)，老师对学生的作业指导（tutorial）[比如论文（thesis, dissertation）或设计（design）]，学生之间对作业的讨论和任务分配 (group discussion, assignment discussion)，学生对课程的反馈以及对老师的评价（course feedback）等。

IV. Word Bank

1. instruction, education 教育

2. cultivation 培育，培养

3. primary education 初等教育

4. secondary education 中等教育

5. higher education 高等教育

6. the three R's 读、写、算

7. school year 学年

8. term, trimester 学季

9. semester 学期

10. school day 教学日

11. school holidays 假期

12. curriculum 课程

13. subject 学科

14. discipline 纪律，学科

15. timetable 课程表

16. class, lesson 课

17. homework 家庭作业

18. exercise 练习

19. dictation 听写

20. spelling mistake 拼写错误

21. (short) course 短训班

22. seminar 研讨班

23. playtime, break 课间，休息

24. to play truant, to play hooky 逃学，旷课

25. course (of study) 学业

26. attendance 出勤

27. exemption 免除

28. re-sit 重考，补考

29. report 报告

30. set exercise 固定的练习

31. reference 参考书目

32. cheat 作弊

33. high distinction 优异

34. distinction 良好

35. credit 合格

36. pass 及格

37. fail 不及格

38. academic performance 学习成绩

39. result 考试结果，考试成绩

40. arts 文科

41. science 理科

42. core books 核心书目

43. first-year student 大一学生

44. freshman 大一学生

45. sophomore 大二学生

46. junior 大三学生

47. senior 大四学生

48. graduate 本科生，毕业生

49. graduate school 研究生院

50. postgraduate 研究生

51. international students 国际学生

52. overseas students 留学生

53. exchange students 交换生

54. visit professor 客座教授

55. associate professor 副教授

56. lecturer 讲师

57. teacher assistant 助教

58. tutor 导师

59. secretary 秘书

60. chancellor 荣誉校长

61. president 校长

62. compulsory education 义务教育

63. bibliography 参考书目

64. plagiarism 剽窃，抄袭

65. compulsory course 必修课

66. optional course 选修课

✥ V. Basic Training

Exercise 2

Listen and write T if the statement is true or F if the statement is false.

1. The college tuition is really high for average American

2. The tuition for the average public university is around $35,000

3. Tuition at the private university is higher than that at the public university.

4. Tuition for graduate students may be even less expensive.

5. The students from rich families can also receive grants and loans.

6. In China college tuition isn't that high so many people are able to go to the college.

7. Students can apply for the loans from the school and pay them back after graduation.

8. Many students in America also take out the loans to pay for their tuition.

9. There are all kinds of scholarships from different sources.

10. Getting a job to pay for the college is the best way pay the debts and get experience for later jobs at the same time.

Exercise 3

Listen and choose the best answer.

1. What does the woman complain about?

A. the boring class   B.changing the class   C.quitting the class

2. In the US, students at most universities _____.

A. write evaluation on the class and the classmates at the end of semester

B. can't criticize the teachers and the course

C. are encouraged to give feedback

3. There are things written on the evaluation. Which one is NOT given in the examples?

A. "Was the reading related?"   B. "Was the lecture well organized?"

C. "Were the handouts interesting and useful?"

4. What do the professors react to what the students say?

A. All the professors pay attention to the feedback.

B. All professor want the class not to be boring.

C. All of them have positive attitudes to the criticism.

5. Which is right about the man?

A. He has never written the negative evaluations.

B. Most of his bad evaluations have actually been the assistant.

C. He thinks the teacher's assistants also need to prove themselves, too.

Exercise 4: Spot Dictation

Listen to the recording and fill in the blanks with NO MORE THAN TWO WORDS you hear.

Education Is A Key [1]

Education is one of the key words of our time. A man without an education, many of us believe, is an 1. _____ victim of adverse circumstances, deprived of one of the greatest twentieth-century opportunities. Convinced of the importance of education, modern states 2. '_____' in institutions of learning to get back 'interest' in the form of a large group of enlightened young men and women who are potential leaders. Education, with its 3. _____ of instruction so carefully worked out, punctuated by textbooks—those purchasable wells of wisdom—what would civilization be like without its benefits?

So much is certain: that we would have doctors and preachers, lawyers and defendants, marriages and births—but our 4. _____ outlook would be different. We would lay less stress on 'facts and figures' and more on a good memory, on applied 5. _____, and on the capacity of a man to get along with his fellow-citizens. If our educational system were fashioned after its bookless past we would have the most democratic form of 'college' imaginable. Among tribal people all knowledge inherited by 6. _____ is shared by all; it is taught to every member of the tribe so that in this respect everybody is equally equipped for life.

---

1   https://www.tingclass.net/show-5753-14938-1.html

It is the ideal condition of the 7. '_____' which only our most progressive forms of modern education try to regain. In primitive cultures the obligation to seek and to receive the traditional instruction is binding to all. There are no 'illiterates' —if the term can be applied to peoples without a script—while our own compulsory school attendance became law in Germany in 8. _____, in France in 1806, and in England in 1876, and is still non-existent in a number of 'civilized' nations. This shows how long it was before we deemed it necessary to make sure that all our children could share in the knowledge accumulated by the 9. '_____' during the past centuries.

Education in the wilderness is not a matter of monetary means. All are entitled to an equal start. There is none of the hurry which, in our society, often hampers the full development of a growing 10. _____. There, a child grows up under the ever-present attention of his parent; therefore the jungles and the savannahs know of no 'juvenile delinquency'. No necessity of making a living away from home results in neglect of children, and no father is confronted with his inability to 'buy' an education for his child.

Exercise 5 [1]

Listen to the recording and write down the only word or a number to complete the sentences below.

1. What kind of student comes to _____? The answer to this is, there is no 'Oxford Type.' Common qualities they look for are _____, enthusiasm and motivation for your chosen area of study backed by a strong _____ record.

2. The University of Cambridge is one of the _____ universities in the world, and one of the _____ in the United Kingdom. It has a worldwide _____ for outstanding academic achievement and the high quality of _____ undertaken in a wide range of _____ and arts subjects.

---

1 https://www.tingclass.net/show-5753-14938-1.html

3. The University of Sydney was the _____ to be established in _____ and, after almost _____ of proud achievement, still leads in innovation and quality. The university _____ in sport and social activities, debating, drama, music and much more.

4. Known for _____ in teaching, research, and service to the community, the University of Victoria serves approximately _____ students. It is favored by its _____ on Canada's spectacular west coast, in the capital of British Columbia.

5. New Zealand's _____ university, the University of Auckland, was established in _____, and has grown into an international center of learning and academic excellence. The University is _____ in the heart of the cosmopolitan city if Auckland and provides an exciting and stimulating environment for _____ students.

6. Founded in _____ Harvard has a 380-acre urban campus with easy access to Boston. It has a total _____ of about _____ students. This university comprises many different _____ such as the Faculty of Arts and Sciences, School of Business Administration and School of Education.

7. Columbia University is an independent coeducational university, which _____ master's, doctoral, professional, and other advanced _____, with an enrollment of about _____ graduate and professional students.

8. Boston University is _____ along the banks of the Charles River. With more than 30,000 students from all over the United States and _____ countries, it is the _____ largest independent university in the United States.

VI. Listening Skill 10—Extensive Listening and Intensive Listening

一、泛听

泛听是指广泛的听，作用是培养英语语感，目的在于在听力练习中以掌握文章的整体意思，要求在听力练习中以掌握文章的整体意思为目的。泛听锻炼的是对素材内容总体把握的能力，更符合听力考试中的中高级考试的要求，而且对于培养英语语感，泛听的作用要大于精听。对于激活大家的耳朵感应能力有很大好处，能让人保持一种新鲜感。因此，从严格意义上说，泛听能力是建立在精听基础之上的。泛听可以先从简单的对话内容，或者是已经阅读过的篇章材料开始，通过调整听力倍速来"磨耳朵"，加快进入语境和反应应答的速度。

二、精听

精听是指听一些很典型的主题明确、内容清晰的英文素材，比如简单的有日常对话，较难的有专题介绍，甚至有学术讨论和专业讲座。精听的作用不仅是打好英语听力基础，而且通过精听练习不仅能够提高听力水平，还能够极大地促进词汇和语法的学习，可以说是一举两得。其目的是精准化听力素材和练习，要求在听的过程中捕捉到每一个词，这对真正打好英语听力基础是至关重要的。

大多数外语学习者会关注网络上发布的视频，如 TED 演讲、脱口秀、新闻采访以及科普视频等，这些属于泛听一类。这类听力主要作用是"磨耳朵"和拓展知识面。另外很多 TED 演讲里的演讲者带有口音，不是 native speaker，不适宜用来精听和模仿。

精听的材料，还是选择 NPR、CNN、CBS、BBC 这类专业新闻媒体比较靠谱，因为其发音正宗、表达完整、语法地道。对于初学者来说，喜欢英音的可选择 BBC Learning English，6 minute English，Spotlight 等，美音初学者可选择 CNN Student News，VOA special English 等。精听要求必须有正确文本对照，大家可以把听抄、听写和速记结合起来，写完以后与正确文本相对照，从而查找听力中的各种错误和问题，这样才能提高。

Tips

BBC Learning English 是世界上最受欢迎的免费的英语语言教材之一。七十多年来，它一直在帮助 100 多个国家 / 地区的数百万学习者成为更好的英语使用者。

BBC Learning English 亮点：

- 职场英语　　　・6 分钟英语　　　・ITV 新闻
- SKYPE 新闻　　・经济学人

✎ VII. Note-taking Practice

Exercise 6: Listen and Copy

1. Well, scores are important in America, too. But it's not the only thing that matters.

_____

2. In fact, college prefers students who have lots of extracurricular activities too, like sports or theater.

_____

3. I don't think deciding solely on the basis of one test is very rational because you could be talented at so many things.

_____

4. There are certainly other ways in which I think the Chinese educational system is better.

_____

5. American education gives students more freedom and puts more importance on creativity.

_____

6. One result is that not as many students choose to work really hard at subjects like math.

_____

7. I mean freedom is important, but not if a good foundation and certain core subjects comes as the price.

_____

8. Well, I think the point is that both systems have their strengths and weaknesses, so both countries have something to learn from the other.

_____

Exercise 7: Listen and Write [1]

1. _____
2. _____
3. _____
4. _____
5. _____
6. _____
7. _____
8. _____

1　闫先凤 编：《听力密码：听见英国》，中国水利水电出版社，2019 年：第 63 页

✒️ VIII. Target Training

Exercise 8

Listen to the recording and complete the sentences below with THE ONLY WORD you hear.

The English Language [1]

1. The English language started life in about the _____ century. The Angles spoke a language called English. This is where the name England and English come from.

2. In the year 1066, England was invaded and their _____ developed the English language even more. People in old days, even Shakespeare, would spell words with different letters and different orders of letters.

3. As _____ books became more popular around the country, an official way of spelling was developed. (e.g. the Christian Bible)

4. The Oxford English Dictionary describes over _____ words, much more than native English speakers will probably only know.

5. English has borrowed many thousands of words from other languages, such as "ketchup" from Malaysia and "tomato" from _____ language.

6. Another influence on the English language is _____. Words that are common in one area can be unusual in another area.

7. Estimates say that about _____ people have English as their mother tongue. But English users are double.

8. But what future will that be? No one knows. English is already the _____ language of many international organisations and businesses.

9. However, many people are worried that children could stop learning their _____ language and learn English instead.

10. English has grown from a few _____ on an island in Europe, to the world's first global language.

---

1   https://www.tingclass.net/show-8483-246857-1.html

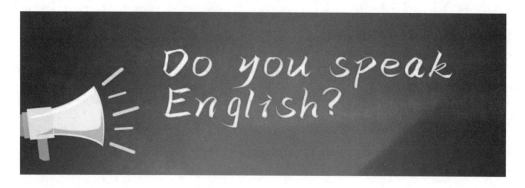

Exercise 9

Listen to the recording and complete the summary below with THE ONLY WORD you hear.

Mitra's Theory About Education—Learning Without Teachers [1]

Sugata Mitra believes that if children have a 1. _____ to know more, then they will learn. He thought about different ways to encourage the 2. _____ of children, even without teachers. He uses 3. _____ to help improve education in the developing world.

On 4. _____, 1999, he cut a hole in a wall of his office to attract the children of the slum. The children soon became interested and without any help, they discovered how to use the machine. In 2001, Mitra started a new project called "Hole in the Wall" to spread his experiment in 5. _____ and India. And he is thinking about new ways for education. In his new project, Mitra works with children in small groups and asks them difficult questions about 6. _____. Usually, the students need to do research and work together without teachers' help.

Mitra believes his methods will help children think about their 7. _____. He also believes that 8. _____ is one way to bring the developed world and the developing world closer together. In a 9. _____ about his work he said, "If cyberspace or the internet is considered a place, then there are people who are already in it, and people who are not in it... I think the hole in the wall gives us a method to create an 10. _____, like a door."

---

1   https://www.tingclass.net/list-8483-1.html

Exercise 10: Preparing for Exams [1]

Part 1

Listen to the recording. Answer the questions with NO MORE THAN THREE WORDS.

1. What scientists from the University of Chicago recently ask students to write about?

_____

2. This study had two parts. Where was the first part?

_____

Choose the best answers.

3-4. What did the scientists do to create the exams for the students? Choose TWO correct answers.

A. They tried to relax the students.

B. They gave the students scholarship.

C. They kept a written record of the performance of every student.

D. The students would watch a film and measure their own performance.

E. They made the students feel more anxiety.

5-6. In the second part, what did the students do? Choose TWO correct answers.

A. They were all asked to write their thoughts and feelings about the exam.

B. They all shared their worries and concerns.

C. They all expressed positive thoughts.

D. They all had worries, but they also felt that they had studied well.

E. All of the students that wrote down their feelings earned higher marks in the exam.

_____

1   https://www.tingclass.net/show-9694-367699-1.html

Part 2

Complete the flow chart with THE ONLY WORD you hear.

Preparing for Exams

As you learn a subject, work to understand it as you learn.

⬇

As the time for the exam gets nearer, make a plan.

- List the material you need to review.
- Then decide the amount of time you will need.
- Find a quiet place to study.

⬇

There are many different ways to study.

- To write your studies using different 7. _____.
- To study with other students in your class.

⬇

On the day before the exam

- study your 8. _____ subject in the morning.
- do physical activities, like sport, later in the day.
- sleep at night.
- do not lie in bed and worry.

⬇

On the morning of the exam

- eat a good meal.
- wear clothes that fit well.
- make sure you do not have to hurry.
- bring everything you need, including extra pens and pencils to write with.

⬇

As the exam papers are given out

- take 9. _____ deep breaths to stay calm.

- read the exam paper carefully.

- choose which questions are easy and answer them first.

- leave more difficult questions until later.

- read what you have written when you have answered the questions.

- 10. _____ what is not clear.

Exercise 11

Learning Styles [1]

Part 1: Listen to the recording. Choose the best answer.

1. When a person knows how she learns best, there are many advantages. Which is the one it **DOES**

NOT have?

A. It will improve his learning efficiency.   C. It will improve his cooperation.

B. It will improve his work.   D. It will improve his competition.

2. Howard Gardner has a famous theory about how people learn. Which one is NOT correct?

A. He thinks that intelligence is the ability to solve problems.

B. He believes there are seven kinds of intelligence.

C. Many teachers don't like his theory.

D. His theory helps us understand why students are good at different subjects.

3. In David Kolb's theory about learning, which one is NOT correct?

A. He thinks learning is based on experience.

B. He thinks that experiences help a person learn best.

C. He thinks that people learn through real experiences or ideas and concepts.

D. He thinks that people learn better by experimenting than observing.

---

1   https://www.tingclass.net/show-8483-247091-1.html

Part 2: Complete the note with THE ONLY WORD you hear.

Visual learners	• learn best by seeing • like pictures and 4. _____ • like 5. _____ • write down things they hear to remember the information
Auditory learners	• learn best by 6. _____ • remember new information best when they hear someone 7. _____ it. • do not write down as much information • also learn by 8. _____ - Talking about a subject with others helps them remember more about that subject
Kinaesthetic learners	• learn best by doing or touching • like experiments - e.g. They may remember more about how 9. _____ works by doing an experiment to create it. • like to explore by using their 10. _____

Exercise 12: Learning and Leadership [1]

Listen to the recording and complete the note below with ONLY ONE WORD.

Education and Leadership

Mario Matos intends to improve life in the whole Dominican Republic through education and training leaders in the local community.

Improving education

• Over 1. _____ people in the Dominican Republic live extremely poor, especially in rural areas.

• As a result, many 2. _____ children leave school early to earn money.

• Without education, children usually stay in poverty.

COCREF (Colegio Christianos Reformados)

• Matos has joined COCREF to improve the situation.

• COCREF now has 3. _____ schools in the country and serves more than 5,000 students from 4. _____ and poor families.

---

1 https://www.tingclass.net/show-8483-250439-1.html

- The COCREF schools are 5. _____ and the schools support each other to offer students a very good education.
- Some students even return home to teach new students or act as leaders in the community.

Helping teachers

- Matos develops better teaching 6. _____ for the schools to help the teachers do their jobs better.
- He also helps the schools and teachers find new ways to reach more students.

Training leaders

- Matos has joined with another organization, The Center for Transforming Mission.

Changing community

- The 7. _____ for changing a community already exists in that community although it can be difficult.
- Many of the leaders are tired and 8. _____ but it is necessary to train and encourage the leaders that are already there.
- Matos and the Center work to do the training by creating 9. _____ of connected people, including over 75 pastors and 10. _____ leaders to care for families and communities in the Dominican Republic.

IX. Listen and Understand the Culture

Exercise 13: Listen, Read and Speak

The Education System in the UK [1]
英国的教育体系

Education in the UK is compulsory for everyone between the ages of five and sixteen. It is provided by two kinds of schools: government and private. Private schools are considered better than government schools but are usually quite expensive.

在英国每个年龄在 5~16 岁之间的孩子必须接受义务教育。这种教育由两种学校提供：公立学校和私立学校。私立学校被认为比公立学校好，但是通常都很贵。

Kindergarten. At the age of three or four, many children start at nursery schools or kindergartens. Here children do not learn any subjects. Instead they learn how to play with other children in preparation for school.

幼儿园。很多孩子在三四岁的时候开始上托儿所或幼儿园。孩子们在这里不学习任何科目。相反，他们学的是如何与其他孩子一起玩耍，为上学做准备。

Primary. Children start their formal education at five. In primary school, students learn the basic skills and knowledge that they will need for the rest of their education.

小学。孩子们 5 岁开始接受正式教育。在小学里，学生们学习他们在以后的教育中需要用到的基本技能和知识。

---

1 http://www.kekenet.com/gaokao/201608/455081.shtml

Secondary. At eleven, students enter secondary school. They take the state exams or GCSEs (General Certificate of Secondary Education) at the age of sixteen. Students take between 8-12 GCSEs in a range of subjects that always include mathematics, science, English, and at least one foreign language.

中学。11 岁时，学生们进入中学。他们在 16 岁时参加全国考试或 GCSEs（中等教育普通证书）的考试。学生们参加 8-12 门一系列学科的 GCSE 考试，通常包括数学、科学、英语，还有至少一门外语。

Further Education. Students may legally leave school and find a job at the age of 16. However, most students continue into further education. Students who pass 5 or more subjects at GCSE can go to a Sixth-Form college for another two years to study GCEA levels (General Certificate of Education Advanced Level). Most students study three or four subjects at A level. They must work very hard because good A level results are needed to get into a good university.

在 GCSE 继续教育。学生们在 16 岁就可以合法离开学校，找一份工作。不过，大多数的学生会继续接受进一步的教育。考试中通过 5 门或以上科目的学生可以去六年级学校再学习两年的 GCEA 水平课程（高等教育普通证书）。大多数学生学习 3-4 门高级水平的课程。他们必须很努力学习，因为进入一所好的大学需要高级水平的好成绩。

Some students decide to go to Further Education colleges and study more vocational courses. These might include subjects like photography, design or even building and carpentry. These courses are less academic and are designed to train students for a specific career. Most of these courses take about two years.

一些学生决定去进修学院，学习更职业化的课程。这些课程可能包括摄影、设计甚至建筑和木工。这些课程理论较少，专为训练学生从事一份特定的职业而设计。这些课程大部分需要两年时间。

Higher Education. Most students enter university at 18 years old, although many students decide to take time out from study after finishing A levels and usually start at university a year later. More and more students nowadays are entering higher education in the UK, and about one in three people now go to university. Students at university study for a degree. A degree course lasts three to four years. After a degree, a student can continue their studies by taking an MA or a PhD. But, most students finish their studies after completing their degree.

高等教育。大部分学生 18 岁进入大学，虽然很多学生决定完成高级水平学习后暂停学习，通常在一年后开始上大学学习。现在，英国越来越多的学生接受高等教育，大约每 3 人中有 1 人上大学。大学生们为获得一个学位而学习。一个学位课程要 3-4 年。获得学位之后，学生可以继续学习，获得硕士学位或博士学位。但是大多数学生获得学位之后就结束了他们的学业。

What have you learnt from this passage?

1. New words

_____

_____

_____

2. Summary

_____

_____

_____

3. Your opinion

_____

_____

_____